Noel, Diane & David,                                    13/10/00

My family across the pond!
Thank-you for the effort and
support put forth to help
me to realize my dream
of reaching the UK! Especially
thanks for your open arms which
are welcoming me!
       Love you Guys
          Shell

# ABOVE CANADA
## THEN&NOW

*"A man sits alone with a book,*
*the whole world around him grows silent,*
*a voice so secret it can't be heard, just felt,*
*is whispering to him and leading him deep into*
*the world of the greatest wonder and power*
*his own imagination."*

Morley Callaghan
Callaghan's, "My Love for Miracles of the Imagination", More than Words Can Say: Personal Perspectives on Literacy (1990)

To: Tony Owen, Gary McCartie and Jim Pattison
Thanks for setting me on fire.

Magic Light Publishing
Ottawa

Canadian Pacific freight train following Thompson River in central British Columbia.

*"There was a time in this fair land when the railroad did not run,*
*When the wild majestic mountains stood alone against the sun,*
*Long before the white man and long before the wheel*
*When the green dark forest was too silent to be real."*

Gordon Lightfoot 1967
*These are the opening lines of composer and singer Gordon Lightfoot's moving ballad "Canadian Railroad Trilogy".*

# ABOVE & CANADA
## THEN & NOW

By: John McQuarrie

Published by:   Magic Light Publishing
                John McQuarrie Photography
                192 Bruyere Street
                Ottawa, Ontario
                Canada, K1N 5E1

                (613) 241-1833
                FAX: 241-2085
                e-mail: mcq@magma.ca

For reproduction of John's photographs
call Love Visuals at:
(613) 824-8608
e-mail: love@magma.ca

Design:         Dave O'Malley and John McQuarrie
Production:     Diane Donaldson, Aerographics
Printing:       Digital Prepress & Printing Professional Ltd.
                Hong Kong


Canadian Cataloguing in Publication Data


McQuarrie, John, 1946-
Above Canada: then and now


ISBN 0-9699761-6-X


1. Canada—Aerial photographs. I. Title


FC59.M32 1999 917.1'0022'2 C99-900930-3
F1017.M24 1999
Printed and bound in China

# Newfoundland & Labrador

*"Canada Begins Right Here."*

Sign at the eastern terminus of the
Trans Canada Highway, near
St. John's City Hall. Mile 0/Kilometre 0

# Introduction

Very few of us can remember a time before there were airplanes. And no one holding this book was around for the invention of the camera. But this country has been here for 130 odd years – if we start the clock at Confederation. So, for those early years, aerial photography was not possible. But that didn't stop those first settlers from looking up and imagining what the birds soaring over an emerging Canada could see. And a few of them were so intrigued they let their imagination flow through pen and brush to paper, and it is through their eyes that we will begin our magic carpet ride over nearly two centuries of growth.

The camera came along by the middle of the last century. Following the Wright Brothers, the Silver Dart and the Great War, the Royal Canadian Air Force began aerial photography of Canada in earnest, and our first aerial photographic views date from the early 1920's.

Over the past two years it has been my great pleasure to photograph this wonderful country from coast to coast. I concentrated on the more densely populated stretch that roughly follows the Trans Canada Highway and, with help from several great Canadian photographers, augmented my stock of images to give you a rich blend of contemporary aerial views sprinkled with an incredible selection of archival photographs and illustrations.

You are about to embark on a 15,000 mile magic carpet ride over one of the greatest nations on this earth. We will fly at altitudes of between 500 and 1,000 feet and you will control the air speed. No inflight movies or meals, but we will throw in some time travel detours and a smattering of relevant quotations from famous and not-so-famous people that we hope will add to your pleasure during our journey.

Ladies and gentlemen, we have just received our take-off clearance so please fasten your seatbelts and enjoy the flight!

John McQuarrie
Ottawa

Cape Spear, Newfoundland

Cape Spear Lighthouse

## Cape Spear National Historic Site

Built in 1835, the Cape Spear Lighthouse is the oldest existing lighthouse in Newfoundland. The two-story, wooden structure that served as a marine beacon from 1836 to 1955 is now a lifestyle museum operated by Parks Canada. The second, conical, stone lighthouse visible along the ridge to the right of the original building, is an automated facility maintained by the Canadian Coast Guard. The site is also an excellent vantage point from which to view whales and icebergs.

And should your robust spirit of adventure take you to this wind swept point before sunrise – and the weather gods are on your side – you will be the first human being privileged to see the sun rise out of the Atlantic that morning. This as you will be standing on the eastern-most tip of the North American land mass.

*"The service we render to others is really the rent we pay for our room on earth."*

Sir Wilfred Grenfell
*Grenfell administered to the medical needs of the outporters of Newfoundland and Labrador. This quotation comes from his A Labrador Logbook (1938)*

*"Such is the nature of this city: windy, fishy, anecdotal, proud, weather-beaten, quirky, obliging, ornery, and fun."*

Jan Morris, Anglo-Welsh travel writer, Saturday Night, March 1989.

*Queen's Battery, perfectly situated to discourage hostile seafarers from entering the inner harbour.*

*"See you in London."*

John Alcock 1919
*Last words uttered in public by the daring pilot on June 14th, 1919,
minutes before the English aviator took off, with co-pilot Arthur
Whitten Brown, from St John's, Newfoundland for Clifden, Ireland.*

*In the bird's eye view above we see how an artist's imagination allowed nineteenth century citizens to see their St. John's from the air, years before the invention of the airplane.*

# St. John's

For more than 500 years, explorers, adventurers, pirates and all manner of seafarers have made their way to St. John's' naturally sheltered harbour. According to popular tradition, the harbour's first European visitor was John Cabot in 1497, although the exact location of his first landfall is still a topic of debate. Claimed for the British Empire in 1583 by Sir Humphrey Gilbert, St. John's is the oldest and most easterly port city in North America and is today, with a population of 175,000, the provincial capital of Newfoundland and Labrador.

The contemporary aerial view at left shows just how beautifully Mother Nature created this protected harbour for the future city. The Narrows, flanked by Fort Amherst at its southern entrance and the massive Signal Hill (National Historic Site) standing guard on the northern flank, ensured safety from all manner of invaders for the earliest residents. St. John's' most famous landmark, Cabot Tower, can be seen at the top of the hill. Built in 1897 in honour of Queen Victoria's Diamond Jubilee, and the 400th anniversary of John Cabot's "Voyage of Discovery", the Tower was used for signaling until 1960. Today it houses Parks Canada exhibits describing the tower's history. Visitors also learn that this was the site where Marconi, in 1901, received the first transatlantic wireless signal.

*The entrance to St. John's Habour and Signal Hill (right center).*

*"The only thing wrong with Confederation is that we didn't join in 1867."*

J.R. (Joey) Smallwood 1949
*Joey Smallwood became the first Premier of Newfoundland when the country that he loved so much – he called it "this poor bald rock" – joined Confederation on April 1st, 1949. He was quoted by Richard Gwyn in Smallwood: The Unlikely Revolutionary (1968)*

*Tourists leaving the Narrows aboard the tour boat Scademia for a sun-filled afternoon exploring Newfoundland's coastline from the open Atlantic.*

*"Then hurrah for our own native isle, Newfoundland!*
*Not a stranger shall hold one inch of it strand!*
*Her face turns to Britain, her back to the Gulf.*
*Come near at your peril, Canadian Wolf!"* —

Folk Song 1869
*Newfoundlanders resisted the appeal of Confederation from 1867 to April 1st, 1949, when Newfoundland became Canada's tenth province. This song was popular during the election of 1869 when Newfoundlanders voted against Confederation with Canada.*

Fort Amherst standing guard on the south side of the Narrows, the channel leading into St. John's' inner harbour.

"'Unnatural' is the key word. Winter is not natural. There's a perfectly good reason it is silent out there. Anything with legs or wings and two brain cells to rub together has left – that's why it's silent. Robins, Canada Geese, Scarlet Tanagers, Canaries, Monarch butterflies – do you hear them warbling about the eerie, haunting, silent unnatural beauty of a Canadian winter?"

Arthur Black, broadcaster, "Winter," *Basic Black: The Wit and Whimsy of Arthur Black* (1981).

*Western Brook Pond in the depths of Newfoundland's winter*

*Western Brook Pond in summer. (Newfoundlanders refer to fjords as 'ponds') Photo: Barrett & MacKay (applies to both shots)*

## Gros Morne National Park

One of Parks Canada's true crown jewels, Gros Morne National Park, on the far western side of the island, was declared a UNESCO World Heritage Site. Al the superlatives we toss around too freely in describing our personal magic places do not come close to capturing the essence of this place.

The scenery is spectacular: deep fjords carved by glaciers, flat-topped mountains of rare rocks and tundra, sea stacks just offshore, even sand dunes. Here geologists found proof of the theory of continental drift in rocks usually found only deep within the earth's mantle.

*"A land may be said to be discovered the first time a European, preferably an Englishman, sets foot on it."*

Vilhjalmur Stefansson 1964
*This explorer was regarded as controversial and outspoken for uttering sentiments like the one above. It comes from his autobiography, Discovery (1964). In the intervening years, the traditions and sentiments of the native peoples and ethnic minorities have been asserted, so that today the remark may sound obvious rather than outspoken.*

*Heart's Content, a small village that takes its delightful name from one of three ships that brought a group of English settlers into Trinity Bay around 1830. Immediately south you will find the other two: Heart's Desire and Heart's Delight. Heart's Content has the additional distinction of being the site where the first transatlantic cable was landed in 1866.*

*Petty Harbour is a lovely example of Newfoundland's outports. Located only 18 kilometers south of St. John's, it's scenic nature has been discovered by film makers. Canadians may remember Farley Mowat's A Whale For The Killing, which was filmed here.*

*Scenic Highway 80 winds it way south along the coast of Trinity Bay just north of Heart's Content.*

Trout River, a fishing village located on the west coast within the magnificent Gros Morne National Park. Photo: Barrett & MacKay

*"I'se the b'y that builds the boat,*
*And I'se the b'y that sails her!*
*I'se the b'y that catches the fish*
*And takes 'em home to Lizer."*

Folk Song 1950s
This is the first verse of "I'se the B'y", a very popular
Newfoundland song, one that is well-known across Canada.

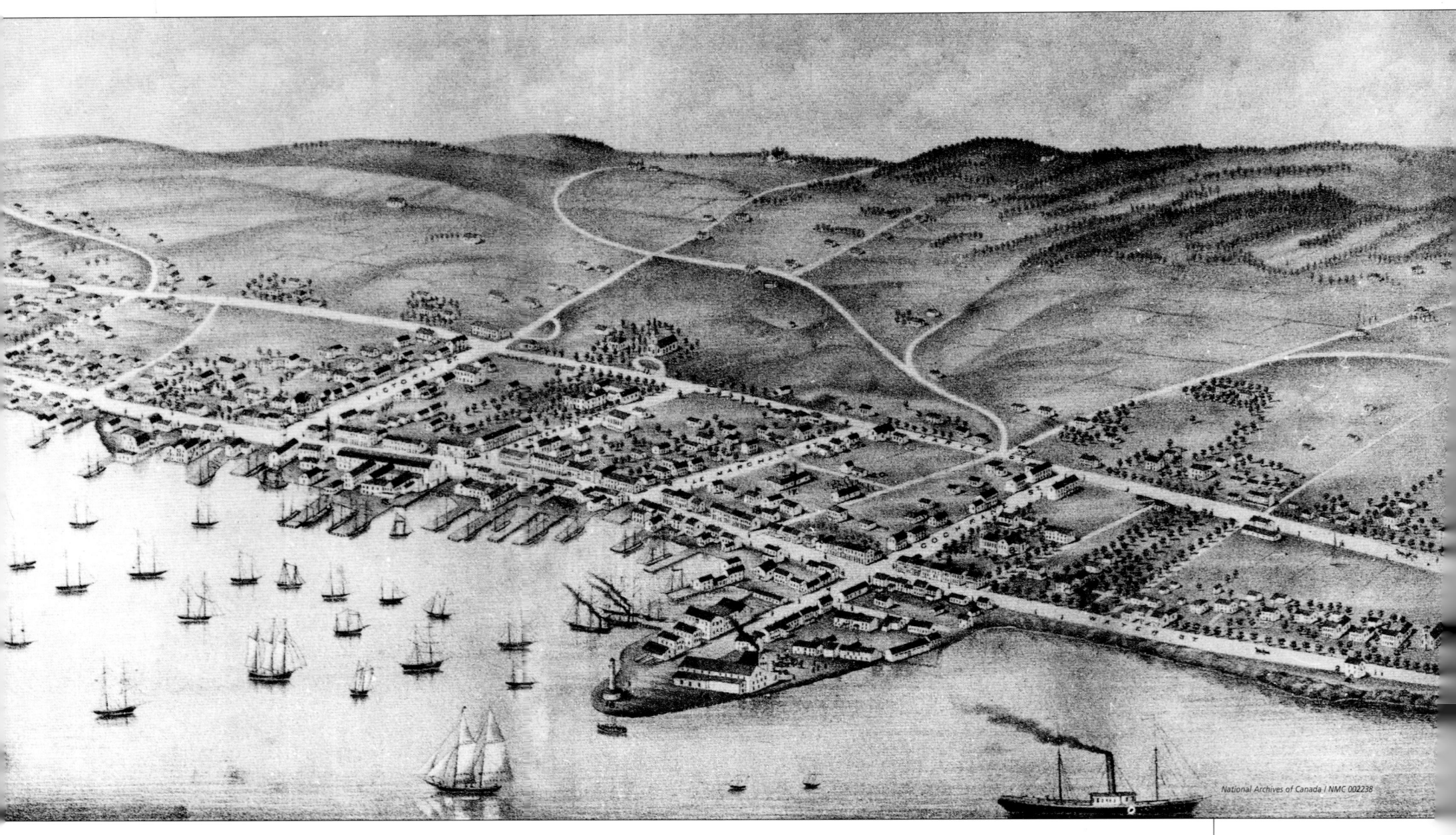

*Bird's eye view of Harbour Grace in 1879.*

"The Aire in Newfound-land is wholesome, good;
The Fire, as sweet as any made of wood;
The Waters, very rich, both salt and fresh;
The Earth more rich, you know it is no lesse.
Where all are good, Fire, Water, Earth, and Aire,
What man made of these foure would not live there?"

Robert Hayman 1628
These charming lines, descriptive of Newfoundland, come from Quadlibets (1628), the first book of original verse written on the continent of North America.
It was composed by Robert Hayman, Governor of the Colony at Harbour Grace, Conception Bay, Nfld.

The contemporary view of Harbour Grace shows the town has changed in over a century but, then again, not all that much perhaps...

# Nova Scotia

*Farewell to Nova Scotia, the sea-bound coast!*
  *Let your mountains dark and dreary be,*
*For when I am far away on the briny ocean tossed*
  *Will you ever heave a sigh and a wish for me?*

Folklorist Helen Creighton collected this sailor's lament in rural Nova Scotia in the 1930s. It became the theme song of the Halifax-based, CBC-TV show "Singalong Jubilee" in 1961, and it was memorably recorded by Catherine McKinnon.

*Snug harbour at Peggy's Cove*

# Peggy's Cove

Peggy's Cove, named after the sole survivor of an 18th century shipwreck, is a uniquely rugged fishing community centred around a narrow ocean inlet and dominated by the famous lighthouse, perched high up on a huge, wave-washed granite point. Peggy's Cove light is no longer an operating beacon, but now serves as Canada's only post office located in a lighthouse. The post office has its own stamp cancellation – an image of the lighthouse.

*Lighthouse and point at entrance to harbour.*

*"Heaven is my home doubtless. But Halifax is my haven."*

Bliss Carmen 1928. *Poet at reception in Halifax.*

(1935) Public Archives of Nova Scotia / 466 - 53,1

# Halifax

In 1999 Haligonians celebrated their 250th anniversary of the founding of their city-by-the-sea in 1749. Strolling amidst the restored piers and privateer's warehouses dotting the beautifully restored Historic Properties, one can't help but feel the pulse of one of Canada's truly magnificent cities, with its proud, seafaring heritage. Halifax's harbourfront is alive with open park areas, public wharves, museums, shops, seafood restaurants, a casino and a never-ending parade of people soaking up the sun, sights and sea smells along the boardwalk.

A personal note: Apart from flying, one of my favourite things to do is walk. All Canadian communities have one – their Canadian Experience Walk. Vancouver has its sea wall, Winnipeg its Forks, Toronto its Harbourfront, Montreal its Old Port and Halifax its glorious Waterfront Boardwalk. If you want to make a day of it, start with The Citadel (following pages). Then its a downhill stroll to the waterfront. Get an attractions list at the visitor center, a lobster roll at Harbourfront and, over your most Nova Scotian of lunches, plan the afternoon. Must sees include the Bluenose II if she's in town, the Maritime Museum, including a tour of the Sackville (a W.W.II RCN Corvette), and the newly opened Pier 21, Canada's Ellis Island. And there is nothing like finishing the day with a plate of clams and a pint of Keith's at Salty's.

*Four views of Halifax Harbour and the area of shoreline that has been re-developed today into the "Historic Properties".*

*Halifax waterfront, 1935. Inset Halifax in 1890.*

(1923) National Air Photo Library / K4 9.14

*Two views (1923 and 1999) looking north into Halifax Harbour. Halifax is on the left with Dartmouth to the right and George's Island in the foreground of the contemporary photograph. Bedford Basin, staging area for the huge convoys of W.W.II, can be seen at the top of both photos.*

*Two views (1929 and 1999) of Halifax looking east over The Citadel and Harbour towards Dartmouth. If you look closely at both of the old photos you may be able to pick out the Dartmouth-Halifax ferries churning back and forth. They have been doing this same trip every single day since 1752, making them possibly the oldest salt water ferry crossing in North America.*

(1929) National Air Photo Library / A1238.35

# The Citadel

High above Halifax sits a star-shaped citadel, one of the great British fortifications of the 19th-century. Operated by Parks Canada, the Halifax Citadel is recognized as one of the most visited historic sites in Canada. A living history program of interactive exhibits, this cultural treasure is a constant reminder of the city's past and endures as a gateway to Canada's colonial heritage and passage to nationhood.

*"England would be better off without Canada; it keeps her in a prepared state for war at real expense and constant irritation."*

Napoleon Bonaparte 1817

*Canada's East Coast Navy*

Canada's Navy operates from two bases in Canada. HMC Dockyard is home to the Atlantic Fleet while the Pacific Fleet is based at Esquimault just north of Victoria, British Columbia.

The top photo at right shows a Sea King helicopter's highly choreographed approach for landing aboard the flight deck of HMCS Skeena. Since the photo was taken, this ship, and the remaining St. Laurent and Tribal classes of ships have been 'paid off' (decommissioned), and replaced with the ultra-modern fleet of City Class Patrol Frigates built in Canada.

The middle photo reflects the three basic classes of ships operated by today's modern Navy. At the top are two Canadian Patrol Frigates, in front of these can be seen three Maritime Coastal Defense Vessels and the large ship to the left is a replenishment ship.

The bottom photo shows the Bedford Institute of Oceanography across the harbour in Dartmouth. Science-tasked ships of the Canadian Coast Guard can be seen tied up alongside the Institute's docks.

*HMC Dockyard naval base and the Angus L. MacDonald Bridge over Halifax Harbour.*

When Canadians conjure up thoughts of Atlantic Canada, the type of images that come to mind are often very much like those you see on these pages. To the left is Cape d'Or Lighthouse perched on a ledge high above the point where the Bay of Fundy runs into the Minas Channel. While the light is now automated, the former lightkeepers' homes have been converted to interpretive centre, tea room & guest house.

Oak Island has been, since the discovery of a mysterious system of tunnels and shafts in 1795, a source of legend and rumour of pirate gold. Two centuries of treasure hunters, including American President Franklin D. Roosevelt, have failed to solve the mystery. Invariably, any excavation is suddenly inundated with water. The swampy hole visible at this end of the island is mute testimony to this difficulty. The island is closed to the public. Sambro Island, near the entrance to Halifax Harbour, is home to North America's oldest operating lighthouse, built in 1759.

Oak Island

Sambro Island

Lobster Bay

Lobster Bay

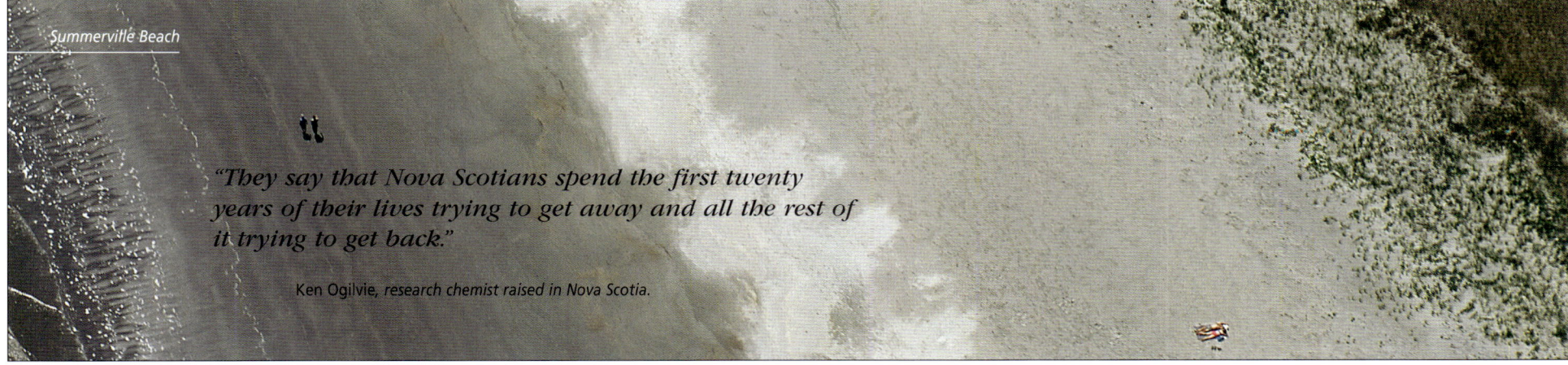
Summerville Beach

*"They say that Nova Scotians spend the first twenty years of their lives trying to get away and all the rest of it trying to get back."*

Ken Ogilvie, *research chemist raised in Nova Scotia.*

South Shore

# Cape Breton Island

*"I have traveled around the globe. I have seen the Canadian and the American Rockies, the Andes and the Alps and the Highlands of Scotland; but for simple beauty, Cape Breton Island outrivals them all."*

Alexander Graham Bell, *inventor and resident of Cape Breton Island.*

*Lobstermen returning to port.*

Cape Breton Island surprises everyone the first time they cross the short causeway from Canso linking the island to mainland Nova Scotia. First she is home to the Province's only mountains and, while they do not compete with the Canadian Rockies, they have a charm all their own, reminding all who have been to Scotland of that lovely country. Indeed, a drive up the coast to Cape Breton Highlands National Park often causes tourists to think they have been mystically transported to the Scottish Highlands. This after place names like Inverness, Creignish, Craigmore, Campbell and Glenora reflect the area's strong Scottish heritage. And this latter town is home to North America's only Single Malt Whisky Distillery.

*Bird Island near mouth of St. Ann's Bay*

*Forested carpet of Cape Breton Highlands National Park*

*Cape Smokey on the Cabot Trail, just south of the lovely seaside village of Ingonish.*

## *Magic Lobster*

This is not really a recipe. More like a Canadian ritual. And if you follow it exactly the experience will remain with you longer than most.

**Preparation Time:** Your life 'till this moment
**Cooking Time:** 0

**Ingredients:**
2 market lobsters (1 to 1 1/2 lbs each), cooked
1 bottle of Nova Scotia white wine
1 medium sized rock (about 2 lbs)
1 corkscrew
No butter
No garlic
No salt or pepper

Ideally you will be on a journey through the Maritimes when a roadside sign beckons "Cooked Lobsters". Packed in ice – along with your wine – they will travel nicely for several hours as you search for your private dining place by the sea. Take the first side road where the sign includes the word "wharf". Ideally it will be early evening, your pier quiet, atmosphere just right. Set yourself down on the edge of the dock, lobsters, rock and wine at hand. Gently tap the claws with said rock until they crack and voila, your meal is prepared. Tail and body can be opened with your hands so no utensils are required. As you savour your simple meal from the sea, by the sea – toss the scraps into the ocean where they will not go unappreciated.

Then, let your mind wander, enjoying the lovely places it takes you.

*Blue Rocks near Lunenburg.*

# Bluenose and Lunenburg

*View of Bluenose II and Lunenburg Harbour in 1996.*

*View of Lunenburg Harbour in 1923.*

Ask any Canadian to name things synonymous with Canada and the *Bluenose* will invariably come up right after the Mountie. She has held an honoured place in our hearts since the heyday of her racing career, and on the Canadian dime since 1937.

In 1920, after years of friendly rivalry between USA and Canadian fishing schooners, The Halifax Herald established a formal race series – The International Fishermen's Trophy. Nova Scotians, dismayed that a Massachusetts schooner took the Trophy that first year, commissioned William J. Roué to design a challenger. *Bluenose* was launched in Lunenburg on March 26, 1921 and, after a season fishing on the Grand Banks, won back the Trophy that year – and every series thereafter including the final in 1938.

The Second World War saw the end of the era of the great fishing schooners. In 1942, despite efforts by her Master, Capt. Angus J. Walters of Lunenburg, and others to keep the ship in Nova Scotia, *Bluenose* was sold to carry freight in the West Indies. On January 28, 1946, the Queen of the North Atlantic foundered on a Haitian reef.

On July 24, 1963, the legend was reborn in the form of *Bluenose II*. Built from identical plans as *Bluenose*, in the same shipyard of Smith and Rhuland and by some of the same men, she is owned by the Province of Nova Scotia and operated by the Bluenose II Preservation Trust.

The real beauty of *Bluenose II* is that, far from existing as a static, museum display, the ship spends her summers sailing the waters of Atlantic Canada where people from all over the world can have the wonderful experience of actually going to sea on her for a day sail. For a unique Canadian Experience, this one would be hard to beat…

© Bluenose II Preservation Trust, Web Site: www.bluenose2.ns.ca

Bluenose II taking a group of tourists on a day-sail around Halifax Harbour.

"The wood that can beat the Bluenose ain't been planted yet."

Angus Walters, *Master of the Bluenose*. 1921

Bluenose leading the American challenger Columbia into Halifax Harbour
for her third consecutive victory in the 1923 International Fishermen's Trophy race.

# Prince Edward Island

*"One is not supposed to be sentimental in Canada, least of all in generalization, but at a moment when almost everywhere in the world small nations are rediscovering themselves, I think it high time the Canadians resumed the practice of national pride. For myself I am not ashamed to say that I have grown to love their country, and would like to give it a figurative kick in the pants, to get its adrenaline going."*

Jan Morris, *Anglo-Welsh travel writer, The Toronto Star, March 29th, 1990.*

*Early morning fog hugs the ground at Burlington. Photo: Barrett & MacKay*

Canada's smallest province – 224 km long and from 6 to 64 km in width with a population of 136,000 – is also its most charming. The gentle waves of the Gulf of St. Lawrence lap against the sandstone cliffs of the North Shore. The bays and inlets offer shelter for the fleet of Cape Islander fishing boats and tree-lined clay roads divide the rolling fields of clover and her world-famous potatoes. Striking reds, greens and blues awaken the senses and a memory lies around every corner.

*Cormorants and lobstermen go about their early morning business off Orby Head. Photo: Barrett & MacKay*

*"And it may be said that here, on little Prince Edward Island was that union formed which has produced one of the greatest nations on the face of God's earth."*

Thomas Heath Haviland, *Father of Confederation, c. 1864.*

Aerial view of Charlottetown today.

Aerial view of Charlottetown today.

Aerial view of Charlottetown waterfront, 1923.

# Charlottetown

Charlottetown was named after Queen Charlotte, wife of King George III, by Captain Samuel Holland when he surveyed tiny St. John's Island, now Prince Edward Island, in 1765. Three years later the town was laid out and the first two houses were built. Today, one of Canada's oldest cities is home to nearly 40,000 people – almost a third of the province's total population.

Province House, in downtown Charlottetown, was the setting for the famous Charlottetown Conference in 1864, where the foundation for the new Dominion of Canada was laid. Today, Prince Edward Island's provincial legislature continues to meet in the assembly chamber first used in 1847.

Birds eye view of Charlottetown, 1878.

*"When I am asked if Anne herself is a "real person" I always answer "no" with an odd reluctance and an uncomfortable feeling of not telling the truth. For she is and always has been, from the moment I first thought of her, so real to me that I feel I am doing violence to something when I deny her an existence anywhere save in Dreamland."*

L.M. Montgomery *1911, author, journal entry, Jan 27th, 1911, Cavendish, P.E.I.*

*Aerial view of Green Gables site and Parks Canada Visitor Center.*

# Green Gables

Built in the mid-1800s, the house was once the home of cousins of Lucy Maud Montgomery's grandfather. Their farm inspired the setting for her fictional novel, "Anne of Green Gables". The house, grounds and farm buildings portray the Victorian setting described in the novel. Nearby, the Balsam Hollow and Haunted Woods trails feature some of Montgomery's favourite woodland haunts, including Lover's Lane.

*North coast of Prince Edward Island near West Cavindish.*

*Aerial view of Green Gables*

*"Is it the touch of austerity in the Island landscape that gives it its distinctive beauty? And whence comes this austerity? Is it from the fir and spruce? Or the glimpses of the sea? Or does it go deeper, to the very soul of the land? For lands have personalities, as have human beings."*

L.M. Montgomery, *author, letter of September 13th, 1913,*
My Dear Mr. M: Letters to G.B. MacMillan.

*The Links at Crowbush Cove, Lakeside is one of the island's 18 scenic courses offering world-class golf to the increasing number of players coming to the province for its affordable green fees and magnificent views. Photo: Barrett & MacKay*

*View looking east along the Cousins Shore on the north coast of Queens County.*

Couple enjoying Cavendish Beach, Prince Edward Island National Park.

Picnickers enjoying Cape Tryon. Photo: Barrett & MacKay

Shore grill on beach near Seaview. Photo: Barrett & MacKay

Cape Tryon Light, one of over sixty working lighthouses on the Island.

*"Entering the intermediate space between land and sea creates a special mood. With only the relentless rhythms of wave and tide before you, preoccupations of daily life left behind, your worries disintegrate like so many grains of sand."*

Prince Edward Island Visitor's Guide

*"Either you are from Prince Edward Island or you are "from away". And there are only two ways one can call one's self an "Islander". Either you were born here, or everyone who remembers when you moved here is dead!"*
Anonymous Islander.

National Air Photo Library / KA 8.9

*Three views of Summerside in 1923 and 1998.*

*Lobster boats and traps stacked up on docks of Rusticoville and North Rustico.*

*"Now we are all Down Home together. The term has many meanings. If a Maritimer says "Down Home" while sitting in a Toronto tavern, he could be talking of all the Maritimes, or Prince Edward Island or a valley, cove, county, village, or the house where he grew up."*

Harry Bruce, essayist, "Home for Christmas", Down Home: Notes of a Maritime Son (1988).

*North Rustico Harbour in Prince Edward Island National Park.*

*Town of Victoria, on Northumberland Strait.*

*Farm, lighthouse and cottages at sunrise, Birch Point. Photo: Barrett & MacKay*

*Farm, lighthouse and cottages at sunset, Birch Point. Photo: Barrett & MacKay*

# Confederation Bridge

The 12.9 kilometre bridge joins Prince Edward Island and New Brunswick. Opened in 1997, the famous bridge carries two lanes of traffic and takes approximately 10 to 12 minutes to cross at the normal traveling speed of 80km/hour.

*The now deserted ferry terminal sitting for'ornly in the shadow of the bridge.*

# New Brunswick

*"The larger the island of knowledge,
the longer the shoreline of wonder."*

Favourite phrase of the marine scientist and
undersea explorer Joseph MacInnis.

The beacon of Swallowtail light greets visitors as they sail near the bustling fishing community
of North Head. Twenty-four kilometres (15 mi.) long and 11km (7mi.) wide, the island offers
a lot of territory for guests to explore.

*Village of Seal Cove showing the modern Connors Bros. sardine processing plant and, surrounding the small harbour at the top of the photo, old sardine smoke shacks made obsolete by the ubiquitous refrigerator.*

# Grand Manan Island

Thirty-five kilometres (22 mi.) off the coast of New Brunswick at the southern entrance to the Bay of Fundy, lies the Island of Grand Manan – the punctuation mark at the end of the Canada-United States border.

For nearly 200 years, the Grand Manan Archipelago has been home to fisher folk and a quiet hide-away for bird watchers, geologists, naturalists, writers, artists – and recently – whale watchers.

Driven by the famous giant tides of the Bay of Fundy, the water around Grand Manan is nurturing, yet violent. The rich waters are home to an abundant variety of marine life that has kept island fisheries thriving for generations. Beneath the surface lie many a testament the ocean's unforgiving side. Over 300 vessels have been wrecked around the island over the past two centuries.

# Saint John

On June 24, 1604 – St. John the Baptist Day – French Explorer Samuel de Champlain landed at the mouth of a mighty river. In honour of the day, he proclaimed that the river and the harbour at its mouth be named "St. John". Then, in 1762, after several wars, a trading post was established at Saint John and the first permanent settlement in the area was born.

The photo at far left shows the section of downtown officially protected under the Trinity Royal Preservation Area. Known as Prince William's Walk, visitors can experience marvelous examples of ornate Victorian buildings built of brick immediately after the catastrophic fire of 1877 that destroyed 1,612 wooden buildings and leaving 13,000 people homeless. The close-up shows the Market Square area, a large complex of office space, shops, restaurants, a hotel, apartments, a trade and convention centre, the public library, the New Brunswick Museum and a tourist information centre.

*Panoramic view of Saint John looking north from the Bay of Fundy.*

*Downtown Saint John.*

*Saint John's Market Square area.*

*These two photos, the earlier dating back to 1923, show the downtown core. King's Square, one of four laid out in the original town plan, is in the shape of the Union Jack. Beginning at '9 o'clock' and moving in a clockwise direction is the back of the old County Courthouse, Engine House 2, built in 1840 and now housing the Firefighters Museum, the Imperial Theatre at '11 o'clock', the City Market at '3 o'clock' and the Loyalist Burial Grounds at '7 o'clock'.*

*Irving Oil refinery.*

## *A New Brunswick Legend*

When the First World War ended, Kenneth Colin Irving left the Royal Flying Corps and returned to his family home in Bouctouche. After working in his father's general store, he opened the community's first garage and service station in 1924.

Soon after, the Ford Motor Company asked K.C. Irving to open a dealership in Saint John. He also established Irving Oil Limited that same year. It was 1924, and K.C. was 25 years old.

Today Irving stations dot Atlantic Canada and their refinery is the largest volume oil producer in the country, with a capacity of 250,000 barrels per day.

*Ship being loaded with potash bound for Brazil, where it will be made into fertilizer. This facility of the Potash Company of Saskatchewan is operated by Furncan Marine Limited of Saint John.*

# Reversing Falls

*Reversing Falls.*

*Reversing Falls.*

The phenomenon of the Reversing Falls is caused by the tremendous rise and fall of the tides in the Bay of Fundy, which are the highest in the world. In Saint John Harbour, the tides rise 28 1/2 feet so, at high tide the tidal waters are actually 14 1/2 feet higher than the normal level of the Saint John River. The effect of this reversal is felt upstream as far as Fredericton, more than 130 kilometres (80 miles) away. And in the narrow gorge beside the Irving Pulp and Paper Mill the rapids flow upstream during high tide. At mid-tide the water in the rapids is calm for a short time and then, as the tide falls, the flow slowly reverses to the south and, at low tide, the rapids flow downstream. Hence the Reversing Falls. That is the condition evident in these two photos.

*"Canada is an interesting place – the rest of the world thinks so, even if Canadians don't."*

Terence M. Green
*Author, Books in Canada, April 1988.*

*Fishing boat working the Grand Manan Channel in the Bay of Fundy.*

*Commercial fisherman tends to salmon pens in Grand Manan Channel.*

*Real estate values on this island near Grand Manan change with the tides.*

Van Horne Estate

## Van Horne Estate

Just a short drive across the ocean floor – on the bar at low tide only – will take you to the summer residence of that visionary builder of the Canadian Pacific Railway; Sir William Van Horne. Ministers Island is located in Chamcook, near the historic seaside resort town of St. Andrews.

Van Horne named his grand house Covenhoven after his father. It was a huge home with walls constructed from sandstone cut from the shore. It contained some fifty rooms, seventeen of which were bedrooms.

Still standing on the island (top of photo at right), is the gigantic livestock barn which was home to his thoroughbred horses and prized herd of Dutch belted cattle. Among other things it housed a huge hayloft and a creamery where white-coated workers prepared milk and butter. There were also heated greenhouses where such things as mushrooms, exotic plants, peach trees and grape vines were grown.

*"All I can say is that the work has been done well in every way."*

Sir William Cornelius Van Horne 1885
Asked to speak at the "last spike" ceremony, Craigellachie, Eagle Pass, British Columbia on November 7th, 1885, the engineer who oversaw the construction of the Canadian Pacific Railway, made this impromptu remark. Immodest in public manner and achievement, he was personally a modest man. It was Pierre Berton who referred to the construction of the CPR as the realization of "the national dream" in his two-volume history; The National Dream: 1871-1881 *(1970)* and The Last Spike: 1881-1995 *(1971).*

Low tide causeway leading to Ministers Island.

St. Andrews By The Sea

*"To residents, of course, things are already not what they were – where are they, anywhere on earth? To the stranger's eye, though, St. Andrews seems enchantingly frozen in the patterns and postures of its past - a rare survival of quality in the age of trash."*

Jan Morris, *Anglo Welsh travel writer, "New Brunswick"*, Saturday Night, May, 1990.

The Algonquin, a renowned Canadian Pacific Hotel, is St. Andrews' dominant landmark on its spectacular setting overlooking the town and peninsula.

# St. Andrews By The Sea

St. Andrews was settled by United Empire Loyalists in 1783 following the American Revolution. Some of the settlers had dismantled their homes in Castine, Maine and brought them here aboard barges, where they were reassembled and can still be seen today. The main town plan of St. Andrews has been designated a National Historic District and many of its more than 250 homes are 100 to over 200 years old.

# Moncton

Moncton, named after the British officer, Lt. Colonel Robert Moncton, who led the capture of nearby Fort Beauséjour in 1755, was originally an Acadian settlement known as "Le Coude". After the deportation of the Acadians, the settlement lay empty until a group of eight immigrant families arrived from Pennsylvania in June of 1766 with a land grant issued by the Philadelphia Land Company.

Even though Moncton is located 50 kilometres (30 miles) up the Peticodiac River from the Bay of Fundy, its famous tidal Bore causes the river level to rise 7.5 metres (25') within an hour. The contemporary photo above shows the empty river in its low tide state while the 1929 view at right shows a much younger city at high tide. And one can not help but wonder how the tall ship will fare when its supporting river disappears in a few hours.

*Moncton, looking to the north over muddy bottom of Peticodiac River in 1998.*

*Moncton, looking to the north over the Peticodiac River at high tide in 1929.*

## Hopewell Rocks

A *walk on the ocean floor* is what draws people to Hopewell Rocks and its famous "flowerpots", unique pillars of rock created by wind and waves. The people visible in the photo at left are exploring a seabed that will be covered by 14 metres (46') of ocean in a few hours.

Hopewell Rocks

## Fort Beauséjour
## National Historic Park

The French built Fort Beauséjour in 1750 and it changed hands several times during the long period of conflict between the French and English in North America. Located near the town of Aulac at the head of the Bay of Fundy, the fort is open to visitors throughout the year.

*Fort Beauséjour National Historic Park*

# Fredericton

The City of Stately Elms owes its life to the mighty Saint John River that flows through its heart. The river, with its wide, deep waters, was the transportation lifeline that brought people to its rich, fertile banks.

View of downtown looking west.

The town was originally named "Fredericstown" in honour of Prince Frederick, second son of King George III, present day Fredericton. the capital of New Brunswick since 1785 is home to 46,000 people.

In the two photos above – 1929 and 1999 – we can see a few changes have been made to Fredericton's urban landscape in 70 years. While we can be sure that many of the stately old homes hidden in the shade of ancient elm trees are those we see in the contemporary photo, the only really common elements visible in both shots are New Brunswick's Legislative Assembly Building built in 1882 and the old York County Courthouse (bottom right) dating from 1845.

View of western part of downtown in 1929.

*"History teaches us that men behave wisely once they have exhausted all the alternatives."*

Frank McKenna, *New Brunswick Premier.*

View of western part of downtown in 1999.

Downtown core in 1999.

These two photos – 1929 and 1999 – reflect a city that cherishes and protects its historic buildings. Beginning in Officer's Square, the park at upper left, you will see the York-Sunbury Historical Society Museum inside the old Officers' Quarters which was begun in 1839. That's the rectangular building at the end of the walkway leading to a statue of Lord Beaverbrook. Walking west on Queen, the city's main street, running diagonally from the top left corner of both photos, we come to New Brunswick's Sports Hall of Fame, originally the Post Office and Custom House, opened in 1881. Crossing Carleton Street the long building near the corner is the Soldier's Barracks, dating back to 1827. Wilmot United Church is visible at top right and the two small structures on the west side of Carleton, midway down the block to the river, are the Guard House (1828) and the Militia Arms Store (1832). The Pedestrian Way occupies the old bridge approach and ends atop the cement pier supporting the bridge in the 1929 photo. Land reclaimed from the river was devoted to the beautiful, 5 kilometre, 'Green' and 'Riverwalk' framing the downtown area.

*National Air Photo Library / A1237.61*

Down town core in 1929.

## Kings Landing Historical Settlement

Located near Prince William, 34 kilometres (20 miles) west of Fredericton on the beautiful Saint John River, Kings Landing Historical Settlement recreates the sights, sounds and society of rural New Brunswick's Loyalist heritage in the 1800s. This living museum has the largest and finest collection of New Brunswick furnishings, tools and fashions displayed in context.

*Long stretches of deserted beaches help to make the Saint John River a boater's paradise.*

*The Princess Margaret Bridge with Canadian Forces Base Gagetown in the distance.*

# Saint John River Valley

Arguably the most picturesque river in Atlantic Canada, the Saint John explodes through a gorge, swims lazily under the world's longest covered bridge, nourishes Fredericton's charm and culture and, in the autumn, its banks are ablaze with fall colour. The river runs south east with the Trans Canada Highway for company and then drops straight south to Saint John where its water passes through Reversing Falls, entering the Bay of Fundy in grand style.

*"But today he only saw one of the river's secrets, one that gripped his soul. He saw that the water continually flowed and flowed and yet it was always there; it was always the same and yet every moment it was new. Who could understand, conceive this?"*

Hermann Hesse
The German author in Siddhartha on his fictional Brahmin's musing about rivers and life

*The Mactaquac hydro electric dam, completed in 1968, raised the level of the river behind it by almost 60 m (200'), flooding the low-lying part of the valley for more than 80 km (50 miles).*

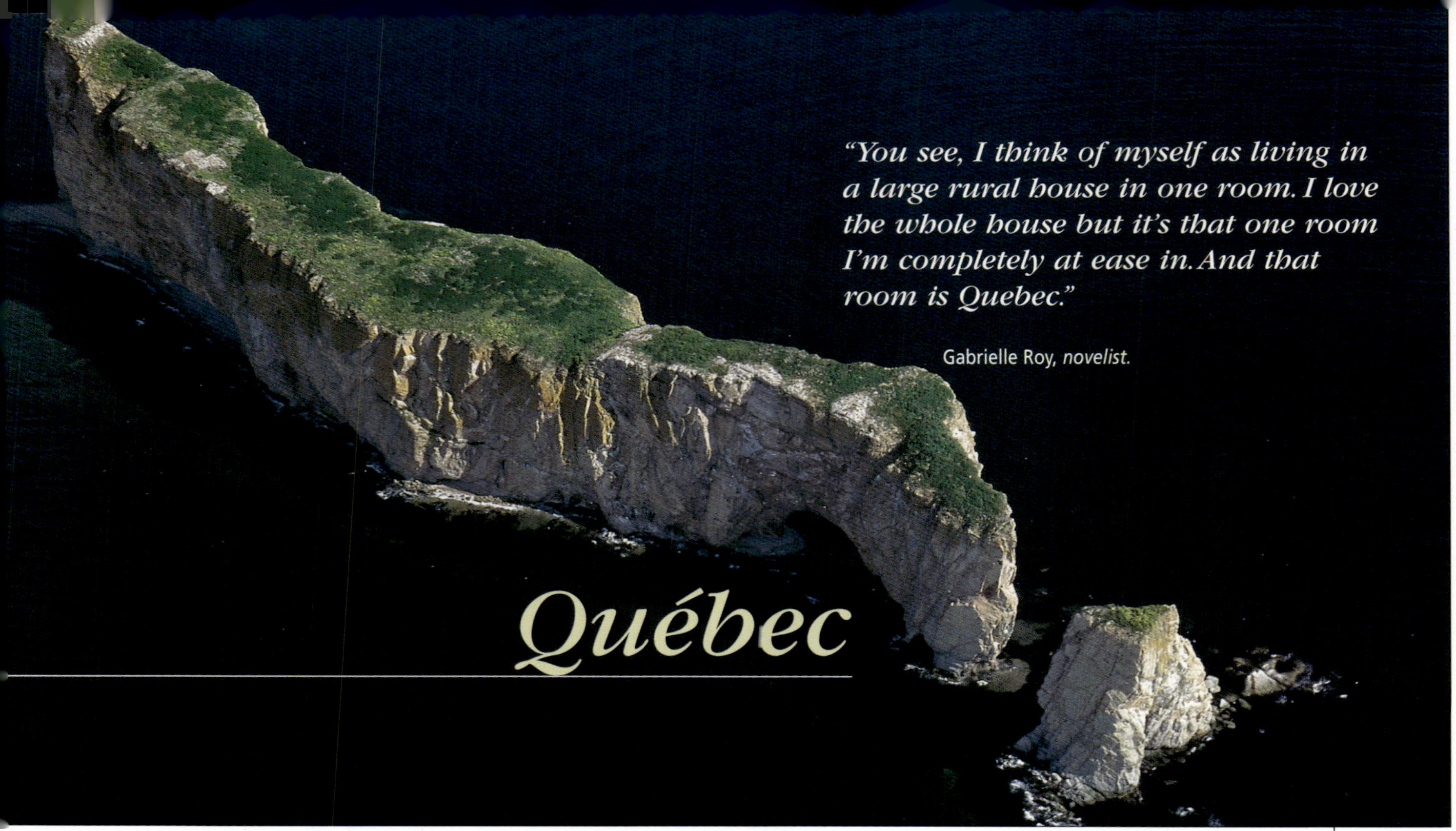

# Québec

*"You see, I think of myself as living in a large rural house in one room. I love the whole house but it's that one room I'm completely at ease in. And that room is Quebec."*

Gabrielle Roy, *novelist.*

*Percé Rock*

With its rich history and deep roots in the past, Québec is an enormous province on a delightfully human scale, where New World vitality and verve combine with Old World charm.

The Québecois are renowned for their joie de vivre. They love to show off their energy and creative talents, and proudly celebrate the distinctive language and heritage that makes this corner of North America unique in so many ways.

*Powered canoe and one of the guides who give uniquely Canadian tours of the Metapedia and Restigouche rivers, noted for their abundant salmon.*

## Gaspé

In Micmac "Gespeg" means "end of the land" but today we associate Gaspé with the beginning of the country and modern history in North America. The cross which Jacques Cartier erected in 1534 earned Gaspé the title of the cradle of Canada.

When people hear the name Gaspé, the image that invariably comes to mind is that of the famous Percé Rock with its signature arch pictured at left. At low tide, visitors can walk out to meet this giant that measures 475m (1500") in length, 90m (270') in width and 88m (275') in height. A remnant from warm tropical seas, the rock's 5 million tons of calcium contains fossils that are some 400 million years old.

Within sight of Percé Rock is Ile Bonaventure, pictured on the opposite page. The island is home to 250,000 birds which nest on the island. Here are cormorants, and a remarkable gannet colony of 70,000 birds.

*Gannet nesting sites and village on Ile Bonaventure.*

# Trois-Rivières

Like many cities around the world, Trois-Rivières emerged from virgin forest at the point where the Saint Maurice River joins the St. Lawrence. Kruger Pulp and Paper occupies an island at the mouth of the Saint Maurice.

*National Air Photo Library / HA302.88*

*Trois-Rivières in 1927.*

*The top, left corner of the large contemporary photo is centered on, and pointing at, the same section of town visible in the 1927 view above.*

*Kruger Pulp and Paper mill.*

"*I never realized that there was history too, close at hand, beside my very own home. I did not realize that the old grave that stood among the brambles at the foot of our farm was history.*"

Stephen Leacock 1925
*This from his address on "The Place of History in Canadian Education," Report of the Canadian Historical Association 1925 (1926). Although his home was in Orillia, Ontario, Leacock was Professor of Economics at Montreal's McGill University for many years and his observation here would apply equally to the family farms pictured here.*

*Strip farms and shoreline along Highway 138, a few miles east of Trois-Riviéres. These long, narrow plots give each farmer that all-important access to water.*

*"I didn't know at first that there were two languages in Canada. I just thought that there was one way to speak to my father and another to talk to my mother."*

Louis St. Laurent 1948
*This Prime Minister from 1948 to 1957, was known as "Uncle Louie" for his avuncular manner. He had a French father and an English mother and was fluently bilingual.*

*Montmorency Falls, just east of Québec City in 1927 and a view from directly above the walkway at the top, today.*

National Air Photo Library / A 611.44

*Montmorency Falls in 1998.*

## Montmorency Falls Historic Site

Located just east of Québec City, in a wonderful natural setting, the Parc de la Chute-Montmorency is a spectacular look-out point over the St. Lawrence River, Île d'Orleáns and the capital city to the west. The spectacular falls plummet 83 metres (272 feet), one-and-a-half times the height of Niagara Falls.

On the western cliff (top left in the large photo) you will notice the Manoir Montmorency. The first building, built in 1781 as a private residence, was used later as a hospital, a monastery and a hotel. Today the manor houses an interpretation centre, a restaurant and a terrace with a panoramic view.

Visitors can take advantage of a dramatic, cable car ascent to the manor, cross the falls on the footbridge and then descend a stairway on the east side, stopping at numerous viewpoints along the way down.

*"Our voices keep tune and our oars keep time.*
*Soon as the woods on shore look dim,*
*We'll sing at St Ann's our parting hymn.*
*Row, brothers, row, the stream runs fast,*
*The Rapids are near and the daylight's past."*

Thomas Moore 1804
*Written on the St. Lawrence River, "The Canadian Boat Song"*
*was penned by the Anglo-Irish poet while a guest of the explorer*
*Simon Fraser in his home at Ste-Anne-de-Bellevue, outside Montreal.*

*Montmorency Falls in 1998.*

73

*Bird's eye views of Québec City in 1905 and 1999.*

# Québec City

Samuel de Champlain saw the potential of this natural citadel, and founded a fur-trading post here in 1608. As religious institutions and government buildings sprang up within the fortifications of the Upper Town, merchants and craftsmen settled in the Lower Town alongside the river. Québec City was a valuable prize sought after many times in the wars of the 17th and 18th centuries. When it finally fell to the English in 1759, New France became a British colony.

Québec, the cradle of French civilization in North America, is today a busy seaport, an important centre of services and research, a cultural hot spot and, of course, the provincial capital. Perched atop Cap Diamant, surveying the St. Lawrence River, the city is one of the landmarks of North American history.

*"Je me souviens"*

Eugene Taché 1883
The motto of the Province of Quebec is "Je me souviens" or; "I remember". Being recalled are the glories of the Ancien Regime – the language, laws, and religion of Quebec before the conquest of 1759. What is interesting is the origin of the motto. It was selected to be inscribed beneath the coat of arms of the National Assembly in Quebec City, February 9th, 1883. The architect Eugene Taché took the words from a three-line poem, which runs like this: "Je me souviens / Que ne sous le lys, / Je crois sous la rose." The poem is of unknown origin; the words mean: "I remember / That while under the fleur de lys (of France), I grow under the rose (of England)". The lines implied co-existence; but in the motto the words suggest separate existence.

## Parliament Buildings

Built between 1877 and 1886 from plans by architect Eugène-Étienne Taché, the Parliament is among the most impressive buildings in the city. The interior and exterior decor reflects the highlights and dominant personalities of our history. This building has housed the deputies of National Legislative Assembly for over a century.

*"The fog lifted and everyone was pointing. A mile or so away was a gigantic fortress sailing majestically along. Pale pink in the setting sun on one side and blue-green on the other. It towered out of the water and with nine-tenths out of sight below the surface, imagination boggled at the size of the whole."*

David Niven, 1932.
The English actor was on his way to Hollywood when he recorded his thoughts that day. The light must have been such that he did not realize the Citadel is perched atop a cliff, and the nine-tenths he envisioned existing below is really just solid granite.

# The Citadel

The largest military fortifications in North America still garrisoned by regular troops, official residence of Governor General in French Canada and home to the famous Royal 22nd Regiment, popularly known as the "Van Doos". Originally constructed as part of the British strategic defense system of North America, the Citadel was built by the Royal Engineers (1820-1832) on the site of the 17th century French defenses.

*View of the Citadel looking to the south east. The south west corner of the old quarter's walled city is visible at upper left.*

*Tourists watching the Changing of the Guard on the large parade square at the center of the Citadel.*

*View of the Citadel looking over the Parliament Buildings toward the glittering St. Lawrence.*

## An Historic Treasure

*Château Frontenac Hotel and Boardwalk overlooking Lowertown.*

*View of Lowertown looking north from over the St. Lawrence River.*

One of Canada's truly lovely places to enjoy a sunny, summer day is the Boardwalk that begins behind the grand old Château Frontenac Hotel, with its medieval-looking gables and turrets. Perched on a bluff overlooking the St. Lawrence River, the overlook offers beautiful views of the water and the historic buildings of Lower Town. In the morning, make your way down and you will find yourself transported back in time to the earliest days of the colony. The whole area, and the adjacent Petit-Champlain quarter, is very much alive with an interpretation centre, many restaurants and bistros, art and craft boutiques and some of the oldest buildings in North America.

After lunch, take the cable car back up and then, a short stroll along the walk, known as Dufferin Place, will bring you first to the Citadel, and then to the Plains of Abraham, also known as Battlefields Park, the site of the pivotal battle of 1759 when the British defeated the French, forever changing the history of the future Canada and the Continent.

*"The Chateau Style is a fascinating anecdote in Canadian architectural history because it was, so far as I know, the only self-conscious attempt ever made to fabricate a distinctive and symbolically significant Canadian style."*

John C. Parkin, *architect, "Chateau and Substance: Towards a Canadian Environment" address, University of Calgary, 1976.*

*View of western part of Lowertown from over the Château Frontenac Hotel.*

*"Is there any city in the world that stands so nobly as Québec?"*

Rupert Brooke, *English war poet who inspired the British with poems reflecting his experiences in the trenches. He died in 1915 of complications from a minor wound.*

*View of Québec City looking east along the St. Lawrence River toward Montréal. Can you find the Château Frontenac, the Parliament Buildings and the Citadel?*

"*You are a grain of mustard seed that shall rise and grow until its branches overshadow the earth. You are few, but your work is the work of God. His smile is on you, and your children shall fill the land.*"

Sieur de Maisonneuve 1642
*This French colonist delivered a sermon-like speech on the founding of the settlement of Ville-Marie, today's Montréal, May 18th, 1642.*

*View of the downtown core looking to the south and east from the area of McGill University.*

# Montréal

The Indian village of Hochelaga originally occupied a site at the foot of the mountain baptized "mount Royal" by Jacques Cartier. Here, in the shadow of the summit, Paul Chomedey, sieur de Maisonneue, founded ville-Marie in 1642. Three and a half centuries later, what was initially a simple missionary village has burgeoned into the world's largest inland port, the home of several of Canada's first banks and trading companies, the world's second-largest French-speaking city, and a metropolis of international repute.

"*Montréal is the only Canadian city with 4:00 a.m. traffic jams.*"

Allan Fotheringham, *columnist*, Malice in Blunderland or How the Grits Stole Christmas (1982)

*Four views of the city showing the downtown core (top) and the area of the Old Port and Old Montréal (bottom).*

Downtown is both the heart of Montréal and one of the most vibrant, cosmopolitan areas of the city. Nestled at the feet of glittering, modern towers, with their spacious contours that reflect the accents of the surrounding gracious Victorian architecture, are a number of the city's most splendid buildings and churches. Countless art and theme museums and charming green spaces dot the area. Light-hearted shopping is only footsteps away on Sainte-Catherine Street and Sherbrooke Street West in the museum district. A broad range of movies, plays and shows draw large audiences, while bars, cafés and discotheques rock until the early hours of the morning.

View of the Port of Montréal in 1904. Montréalers in particular will enjoy the artist's careful 'labeling' of the buildings in his drawing.

These two views, 1923 and 1999, combined with the drawing above, show the astounding growth typical of many of the world's great cities through the course of the 20th century.

> *"And amidst these fields is situated the town of Hochelaga, near to and touching a mountain, which is around it, very fertile and cultivated, from the summit of which one can see far off. We called this mountain "le Mont Royal"."*

Jacques Cartier 1535
*Thus did the explorer describe the site of the Iroquois village of Hochelaga and the future site of the city of Montreal.*

*View looking east toward the business district, with Old Montréal and the Old Port in the foreground.*

Located between the St. Lawrence River and downtown, this historic part of the city and its Old Port will put you into close contact with the past life of this major metropolis of North America, founded in 1642. From fortified town of the 17th century until the first decades of the 20th, Old Montreal has always been the centre of the city, preserving testimonies of all bygone eras. Today, this wonderful, romantic area is a mecca for tourists and locals alike who are drawn to its unique blend of heritage buildings, museums, shops, restaurants, outdoor cafés and riverwalks of the St. Lawrence.

*View of the Old Port and Old Montréal looking north from above the St. Lawrence River.*

*Early stages of construction on the future Jacques Cartier Bridge in 1929. In this view we are looking south from Île Saint Hélène to Longueuil. Seventy years later the bridge is complete and the old Fort Île Saint Hélène has been restored and now houses the Stewart Museum, which tells the history of the discovery, exploration and development of Canada, and its close relationship with the civilizations of Western Europe, which gave it birth.*

*Île Saint Hélène.*

## *Parc des Îles de Montréal*

In the midst of the majestic St. Lawrence River, the Parc des Îsles, an oasis of greenery and gardens a stone's throw from downtown Montreal, is a haven of relaxation and recreation. Montréal's largest park is made up of Saint-Hélène and Notre-Dame islands, the site of the Expo'67, 1967 World's Fair. These two islands offer a huge array of attractions including the Air Canada Grand Prix circuit, the Casino, La Ronde amusement park, The Biosphére, The Stewart Museum, and acres of parkland and beaches.

The Biosphére

This former Expo'67 American pavilion is Canada's premier ecowatch Centre. Dedicated to water, and particularly to the St. Lawrence River and the Great Lakes, the Biosphére is aimed at sensitizing visitors to the importance of protecting these vital resources.

*"Expo '67 is a show that revealed a great new star – the city of Montreal. And Canada has profited from the occasion to emerge in the eyes of the world as a young and determined country looking resolutely to the future."*

Maurice Chevalier, *French actor and singer,* I Remember It Well *(1970)*

Two different roller coasters at La Ronde Amusement Park and the Montreal Casino, all part of the Parc des Îsles complex on Île Saint Hélène.

The four photos on this page reflect 70 years of growth, 1929 to 1999. In the top left image you may be able to pick out Mary Queen Of The World Cathedral and the original Sun Life Building at bottom center. In the contemporary view the (large blue) IBM Building is blocking our view of the Cathedral but the Sun Life Building is still there, but in a much larger iteration.
The bottom photos show a Harbour Bridge nearing completion in 1929, and the Jacques Cartier Bridge, as it was later named, in 1999. Land, reclaimed from the St. Lawrence River is now home to La Ronde Amusement Park.

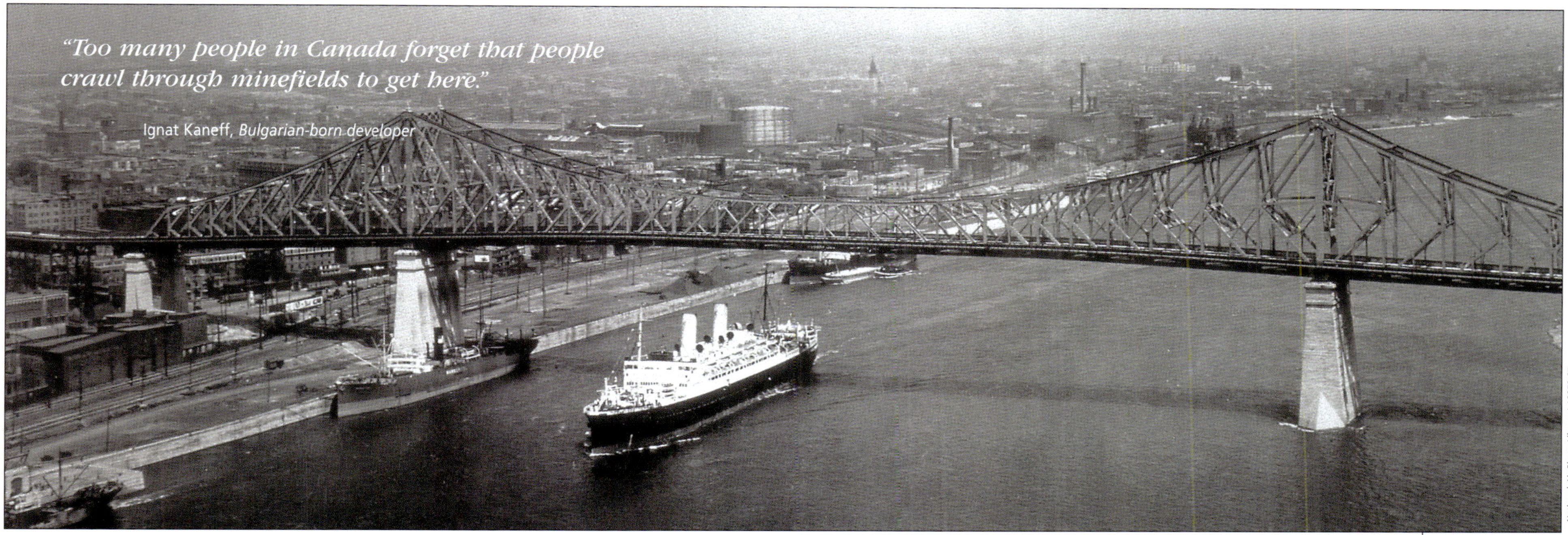
"Too many people in Canada forget that people crawl through minefields to get here."

Ignat Kaneff, *Bulgarian-born developer*

National Air Photo Library / A2272-67

*The year of this photo is 1930, the Harbour Bridge is newly opened and we can only imagine the personal dramas about to unfold for the passengers of the Duchess of Richmond, many of them probably immigrants, as the ship approaches her berth.*

*In these three photographs we see Holland America's "Vandeem" at her berth preparing to get underway, then sailing under the Jacques Cartier Bridge with passengers and crew destined for a holiday cruise to Boston or New York, and a pleasure boat sharing the river with the giant liner.*

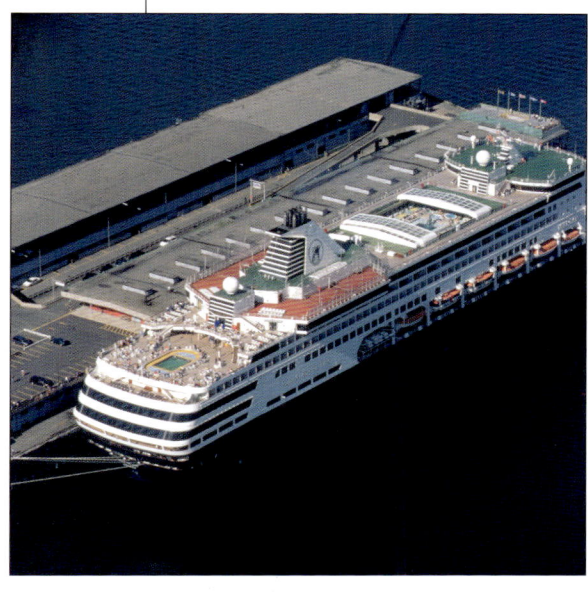

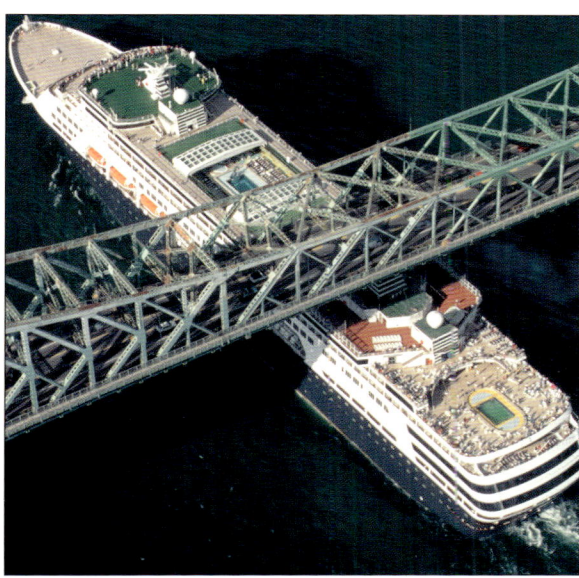

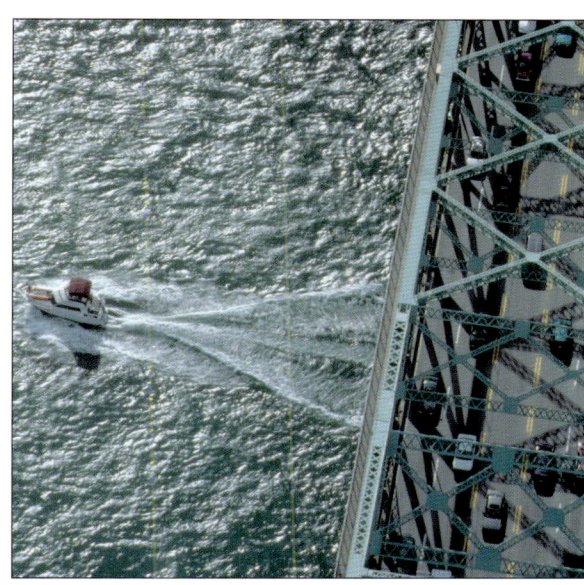

Mary Queen Of The World Cathedral

## Mary Queen Of The World Cathedral

A scaled-down replica of St. Peter's Basilica in Rome, this magnificent Catholic cathedral was built at the end of the 19th century in the heart of what was then the city's Anglo-Protestant sector.

*"This is the first time I was ever in a city where you couldn't throw a brick without breaking a church window."*

Mark Twain 1881
*The American humorist made this remark while addressing a large group of well-wishers at a banquet held in his honour at the Windsor Hotel in Montreal, December 7th, 1881.*

## Saint-Joseph's Oratory

One of the most important spiritual centers in the world, the oratory with its magnificent octagonal dome – second largest in the world after St. Peter's in Rome – dominates the western slope of Mount Royal, attracting over one million pilgrims and visitors a year.

*Hotel and bank towers dwarf lovely Mary Queen Of The World Cathedral. Just across Boul. René Lévesque from the Cathedral we see the stately Sun Life Building. These two landmarks, together with Windsor Station at bottom, are the only major buildings visible in the archival pictures on the previous pages.*

Saint-Joseph's Oratory

*"If some countries have too much history,
we have too much geography."*

W.L. Mackenzie King 1936
*This eccentric, former Prime Minister was, like many of his contemporaries, echoing a common lament of the time for the perceived lack of history a young Canada held in the early years of its existence, when compared to countries in Europe. This so troubled King that he actually built his own contrived ruins on the lovely Mackenzie King Estate that are preserved today by the National Capital Commission.*

*Visitors to the Champlain Lookout in the park enjoying the annual display of fall colour.*

# The Gatineau

Nestled within this broad region located north of Hull and Ottawa, lies Gatineau Park. this wonderful wilderness preserve, which reaches right into the city limits of Hull, offers visitors a complete range of summer, fall and winter delights including both cross-country and downhill skiing, boating, swimming, hiking and, in the fall, the brief but wondrous display of colour that heralds the change of seasons all Canadians must learn to love.

*"In the early October of that year, in the cathedral hush of a Quebec Indian summer with the lake drawing into its mirror the fire of the maples, it came to me that to be able to love the mystery surrounding us is the final and only sanction of human existence."*

Hugh MacLennan 1961
These are the thoughts of the narrator of the powerful novel The Watch that Ends the Night (1961), written by Hugh MacLennan.

*Mackenzie King Estate, Kingsmere.*

*Morning launch of balloons from the town of Gatineau on the Ottawa River during the annual Gatineau Hot Air Balloon Festival.*

*View of the old E.B. Eddy pulp and paper mill and the downtown area of Hull, in the 1950s. Much of this area has since been reclaimed by the Federal Government and is now devoted to park space and the beautiful Canadian Museum Of Civilization.*

*The Canadian Museum of Civilization now occupies the site of the old E.B. Eddy pulp and paper mill visible in the photo at left and below.*

*View of Hull at left from over the Chaudière Falls on the Ottawa River. Ottawa occupies the opposite shore.*

# Hull

The city of Hull lies at the far western edge of Québec, near the confluence of the Ottawa and Gatineau Rivers, where it sprang up with the growth of the logging industry in the early days of the 19th century. Today, with its neighbouring city of Ottawa, Hull is part of Canada's National Capital Region.

## *"Before all I am a Canadian."*

*Sir George-Etienne Cartier 1837*

*The E.B. Eddy plant occupies the islands around Chaudiere Falls in the foreground while the downtown area of Hull, with its Federal Government office towers and Canadian Museum of Civilization, is visible in the background.*

*A favourite angle of photographers and artists since the early days of Bytown has always been from around a thousand feet above and to the west of Parliament Hill. Of course, in this illustration from 1857, Parliament is only in the minds and on the drawing boards of its architects back in Great Britain. The great boiling cauldron of Chaudière, while bridged and lined with mills, is still not dammed. Wrightstown, on the site of present-day Hull, can be seen at lower left.*

# Canada's Capital

Defined by the juncture of three rivers, the Ottawa, Gatineau and Rideau, the area was a natural site for a community. A visionary American, Philemon Wright recognized this and founded his tiny settlement of Wrightstown, on the present-day site of Hull, in the Spring of 1800. But nothing much happened on the opposite shore until Col. John By completed the Rideau Canal in 1826, and founded Bytown.

Though other cities vied for the honour, in 1857 Queen Victoria chose Ottawa as the capital of the United Provinces of Canada, creating a National Capital Region with its unique blend of English and French, that has flourished both as a tourism destination and a government centre.

"On the whole, therefore, I believe that the least objectionable place is the city of Ottawa. Every city is jealous of every other city except Ottawa."

Sir Edmund Head 1857
One reason why Ottawa was chosen to be the capital of the new Dominion was given in the confidential memorandum addressed to the British Colonial Secretary by Governor General Sir Edmund Head.

*In this contemporary view we see the mighty cauldron of the Chaudière Falls has been dammed and a federal government complex of office towers now occupies the site of old Wrightstown. The bluffs of Parliament Hill and downtown Ottawa are visible at the top of the photo.*

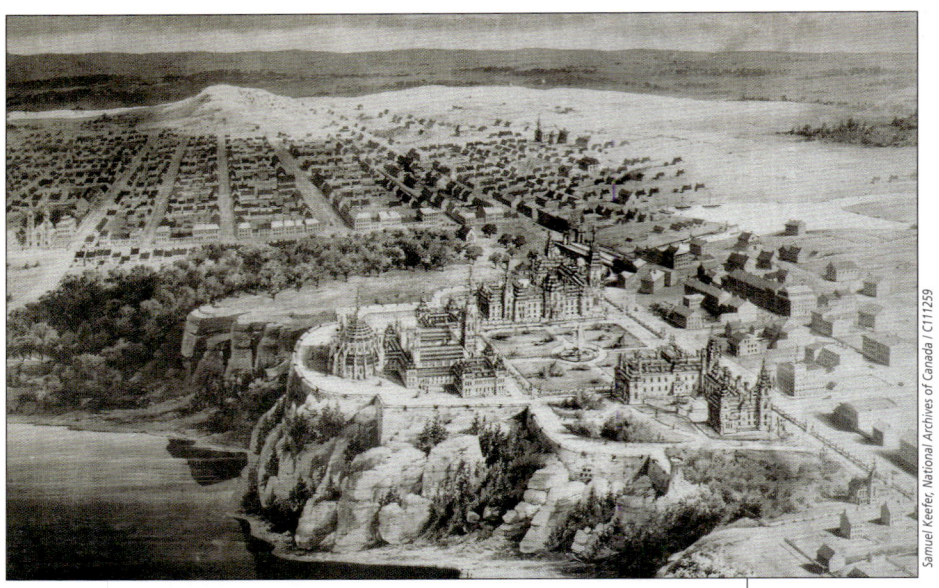

*The "Westminster in the Wilderness", Canada's Parliament Buildings, now lies complete only ten years after Confederation in this view looking east over a very young Ottawa.*

*Contemporary view of the Chateau Laurier Hotel, Rideau Canal locks and Parliament Hill looking to the west.*

*View of Rideau Falls and Green Island in the 1930s. Until well into the 1950s, this area was devoted to industry.*

*Green Island today bears little resemblance to its former industrial focus. From right to left we see the National Research Council Headquarters (bottom right), Ottawa City Hall on its lovely island setting, and the French Embassy (upper left).*

Giant 60-foot hot air balloon in the shape of a Mountie, drifts over "N" Division of the RCMP. In the top left corner we can see the crowd waiting for the beginning of the Force's traditional "Sunset Ceremony" which finishes with a performance of the world famous "Musical Ride".

*"As for the Mounted Police, a few dozen of them managed to maintain law and order over half a continent. Where else in the world is the policeman something of a national symbol and a hero?"*

William Kilbourn, *historian,* "The Peaceable Kingdom Still", Daedalus: Journal of the American Academy of Arts and Sciences, "In Search of Canada". Fall 1988

Hot air balloon in the shape of a mountie drifts lazily across Parliament Hill as long evening shadows creep over the Canada Day crowd gathered to celebrate this most Canadian of holidays.

Changing the Guard ceremony, a daily Ottawa summer ritual, is underway on the lawn of Parliament Hill.

Rideau Hall, home to Canada's Governor General.

# St. Lawrence Seaway

"*Today, this Nation offers to mankind*
*This monument, when the passion in old foes*
*Is blest and sublimated and combined*
*To give Man's utmost for the best man knows.*"

John Masefield, Poet Laureate of Great Britain, wrote this official ode
on the opening of the St. Lawrence Seaway in April 1959.

*View of the western end of Cornwall looking northward across the St. Lawrence. The Seaway International Bridge is visible on the right. The narrow waterway paralleling the river is a remnant of the old Galop Canal, forerunner of the Seaway, and the ruins of one of its locks is a silent reminder of river travel's earlier days.*

*View of Cornwall looking to the north in 1929. Thirty years before the opening of the Seaway, the Galop Canal and locks enabled ships to safely bypass the rapids above the city. The entrance to the canal, visible here, linked up with the portion of the canal still visible in the contemporary picture above. The area of this image is just to the right of the colour photo.*

July of 1999 marked the 40th anniversary of the St. Lawrence Seaway, at 3800 kilometres (2200 miles) the longest inland waterway in the world. It was the marvel of its day, opening the interior of Canada and the United States to ports of the world. Its system of 15 locks raises a ship the equivalent of a 60 story building (200m or 600ft) between Montreal and Thunder Bay at the western end of Lake Superior. But planners in the 1950s did not envision the evolution of super ships and the advent of the container system. These maritime goliaths are much too big to go through the existing locks, so much of the freight that used to travel the Seaway now rides the rails.

Flying over the St. Lawrence, west of the dam at Cornwall, Ontario, many of the old roads, foundations and fence lines of communities and farms that were permanently flooded 40 years ago to enable the existence of this waterway are still clearly visible today, just below the surface

View of Galop Canal just west of the town of Cardinal in 1929.

R.H. Saunders Dam at Cornwall. It was this dam that opened up the river itself to navigation, eliminating the need for the Galop Canal. It also created the body of water that flooded hundreds of homes and farms.

View of St. Lawrence Seaway with remains of the old Galop Canal, and one of her locks in 1999. Cardinal is visible in the distance.

Eisenhower Lock near Cornwall, one of two on the American side of the border.

# Thousand Islands

Typical view near sunset of a few of the famous 1000 Islands near the Ivy Lea Bridge.

Sunday afternoon BBQ on the deck of a lovely island cottage where the guests all arrive by boat

## A Love Story

Romantic Heart Island in Alexandria Bay provides the setting for the saddest of true love stories ever told. In 1900, George C. Boldt, millionaire proprietor of the world-famous Waldorf Astoria Hotel in New York City, set out to build a full-sized Rhineland Castle on Heart Island.

The magnificent 120-room structure was to be a monument of his love for his wife, Louise. Work was well underway, with more than $2.5 million invested, when tragedy struck. In January of 1904, Louise died and Boldt commanded all work on the castle to cease immediately. He never returned to the island, leaving behind the nearly completed castle. For 73 years, the castle and its buildings were left to the mercy of the wind, rain, ice, snow and vandals.

Since 1977, millions of dollars have gone into the restoration of the Heart Island structures. The island and its castle are now visited by thousands of tourists every year. In this photo, one of Gananoque Boat Lines' vessels can be seen moored to the dock.

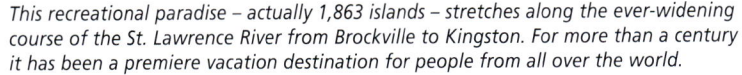

*This recreational paradise – actually 1,863 islands – stretches along the ever-widening course of the St. Lawrence River from Brockville to Kingston. For more than a century it has been a premiere vacation destination for people from all over the world.*

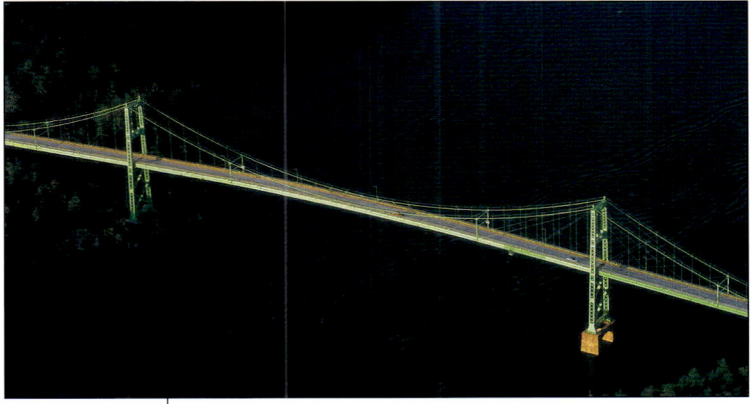

*Ivy Lea Bridge to the USA between Gananoque and Kingston bathed in golden light of a beautiful summer afternoon.*

*Heart Island and Boldt Castle, Alexandria Bay, New York, USA*

*North America's shortest international bridge. The border between Canada and the United States runs under the water right between these two islands. But no sign of a customs house at either end!*

101

# Kingston

Affectionately known as the Limestone City, Kingston is noted for its handsome, 19th-century limestone architecture, surviving examples of which contribute to its distinctive look and atmosphere.

Once the capital of the United Provinces of Canada, Kingston was built on a scale befitting a capital. Its City Hall, 1843-44, is a fine example of the neo-classical style. And its most famous son was Canada's first Prime Minister – Sir John A MacDonald.

Situated at the point where Lake Ontario flows into the St. Lawrence River and at the southern end of the Rideau Canal, Kingstonites enjoy all types of water-related activities in the freshwater sailing capital of North America. And the city is the western gateway to the 1000 Islands.

*Herm Brosius / National Archives of Canada / NMC0022439*

*Bird's eye view drawing of Kingston in 1875.*

*Kingston Harbour in 1924.*

*Kingston Harbour in 1999.*

*Kingston Harbour in 1999. The limestone City Hall and harbour tower are visible at center here and in all three views on the preceding page.*

*Marine Museum of the Great Lakes on Kingston Harbour.*

*Royal Military College (RMC) where students receive a university degree and military training leading to commissioning as officers in the Canadian Armed Forces.*

*Fort Henry, now a living museum was built in 1832 to repel an American invasion that never came.*

*Kingston Pennitentiary in 1999; an operating federal prison for over 100 years*

103

*"I was born in this city. I was raised in this city. I went from this city to see nearly all of the world, and this is the place I want to live and die."*

Gordon Sinclair, *newspaperman and broadcasting personality, opening the CN Tower in Toronto, August 1975, quoted by Scott Young in Gordon Sinclair, A Life… and Then Some (1987).*

*Skyline of Toronto looking to the east. In this view we see the downtown core with its cluster of bank towers, the CN Tower and SkyDome, the waterfront with the Canadian National Exhibition grounds and Ontario Place, visible just beneath the runways of the Island Airport.*

*Built over Lake Ontario on three islands, Ontario Place features an IMAX theatre, exhibits, rides and playgrounds, a marina, restaurants and the Molson Amphitheatre.*

*SkyDome Stadium framed by residential and commercial complexes of the bustling Harbourfront.*

*Canadian Helicopters' medical evacuation helicopter over the downtown core.*

# Toronto

One of Canada's most exciting and cosmopolitan cities, Toronto is the cultural heart of south central Ontario. It's a city of contrasts – the soaring glass and concrete towers of the commercial and financial heart of the country, and the parks, gardens and lakefront boardwalks of a host of communities. It is also one of the English-speaking world's great theatre towns, with dozens of theatres and concert halls, and the world's finest performers on their stages. It's a cultural storehouse, with great museums and splendid galleries.

*Toronto's City Hall overshadows old City Hall.*

Bird's eye view of Toronto looking to the west in 1854.

Archives of Ontario /

National Air Photo Library / HA22.29

View looking directly north from over Lake Ontario in 1920. The golden age of rail is still in full swing as we see the tracks and Union Station (bottom center) dominate in this remarkable photograph.

National Air Photo Library / RA 21.23

The year is 1927 and our viewpoint has moved a bit to the east giving us a north-westerly outlook. Union Station is at left and the Royal York Hotel and Leslie Street Spit are still to come.

*"The entire history of automobiles, airplanes, antibiotics, oral contraception, nuclear energy, computers, plastics, satellites and xerography is encompassed by the span of a single human life."*

—David Suzuki, *scientist and broadcaster, interviewed in Toronto Computers!, March 1990.*

*This 1999 view is to the west. Here the Gardiner Expressway leads us into the very same areas pictured in the three images on the opposite page. The 20th century has been good to this city.*

*Toronto harbourfront in 1949. Opened in 1929, Toronto's landmark hotel, The Royal York dominates the skyline. From the Canada Steamships' wharves we can follow Bay Street north to where the clock tower on the old City Hall is just visible.*

## *Harbourfront*

Harbourfront Centre on the waterfront has developed from run-down warehouses to a thriving cultural, educational and recreational centre. Stretching from York Street west to Bathurst, it combines shopping, recreation and the arts in a lakeside setting of marinas, quays and promenades, boutiques, theatre, restaurants, antique market, art gallery and playgrounds. From here, regularly scheduled boat cruises and private charters will take you on a tour of Toronto Harbour and the Toronto Islands.

*View looking north to Harbourfront and downtown in 1999. Fifty years has made a difference! (Inset) The Royal York Hotel is dwarfed by the surrounding bank towers in this 1999 photo.*

*"Good rich forest land can be bought within a day's journey of Toronto, the capital of Upper Canada, with a population of 16,000, for twelve dollars per acre."*

William Thompson, traveler and writer, A Tradesman's Travels, in the United States and Canada in the year 1840, 41, & 42 (1842)

# The Islands

Established in 1852, The Royal Canadian Yacht Club's current facility on the 'Island dates from 1919 when Edward, Prince of Wales, laid the corner stone for the gracious, southern-style clubhouse that has been the RCYC's summer home ever since. In this photo we see the club in 1925.

Royal Canadian Yacht Club in its tranquil setting with the Toronto skyline only a mile away.

Royal Canadian Yacht Club facility. One of Canada's largest, the RCYC operates a club fleet in excess of 500 boats.

# Toronto Islands

In the summer, people flock to the islands for a day away from the bustle of the city. Only a 15-minute ferry ride from the foot of Bay Street, the islands are a world away from the big city hustle. There's no finer place for a picnic. Wide open, tree-shaded spaces surrounded by water and laced with lagoons make for the perfect spot. There's a farm for kids, rides, playgrounds and boat rentals.

## *"Please Walk on the Grass."*

Tommy Thompson 1960
*The first sign with this message was erected in Edwards Gardens in Toronto in 1960; it attracted national and international attention for its "hands-on" approach. The brain-child of Tommy Thompson, Metro Toronto's Parks Commissioner, it was adopted as the motto of the Parks Department.*

Island Ferry departing for its 15-minute run to Toronto.

*Queen's Park and the Provincial Parliament Buildings.*

*Historic Flatiron building, so-named because of its unique shape, has guarded its location on Front Street since 1882.*

*SkyDome and the new Air Canada Center with Gardiner Expressway and Harbourfront at right.*

*"We must deliver power to such an extent that the poorest working man will have electric light in his home."*

Sir Adam Beck 1908
*This founder and first chairman from 1906 to 1925 of the Ontario Hydro-Electric Power Commission (now Ontario Hydro), made this commitment two years after assuming the chairmanship. He made good on his pledge, electrifying both urban and rural Ontario.*

*Night skyline of Toronto as electric light begins to replace the fading twilight.*

*"The Don River used to run through the Don Valley, which was once one of the most beautiful valleys in all of Southern Ontario. Now the Don Valley Parkway runs through the Don Valley and the Don River hardly runs at all."*

Arthur Black, broadcaster and humorist, "The Not So-Grand River", That Old Black Magic (1989).

*Looking south over the interchange at the juncture of the Don Valley Parkway and Highway 401.*

*View northward of Don Valley Parkway and Bloor Street Bridge.*

*Looking north through the Bay Street canyon to Queen Street. The clock tower of the old City Hall is visible at the top of Bay Street.*

*Ontario's first expressway, the Queen Elizabeth Way, where it crosses Hamilton's Skyway Bridge.*

# Steel Town

Situated at the western end of Lake Ontario, in the heart of the area known as the Golden Horseshoe, Hamilton is a city of contrasts. Its reputation was built on steel. Stelco and Dofasco both have huge steel-making facilities in the city and have shaped its development to such an extent that the words 'steel' and 'Hamilton' have become synonymous for most Canadians.

*View of Stelco's Hilton Works complex in Hamilton. Ship has unloaded its cargo of iron ore pellets destined to be turned into steel by Canada's largest steel maker.*

*Main street of the delightful town of Niagara On The Lake.*

# Niagara-On-The-Lake

This town is the jewel of the Golden Horseshoe, the name given to the region at the western end of Lake Ontario, from Toronto to Niagara Falls. Blessed with a climate more temperate than that of any Canadian city east of British Columbia, this charming town is surrounded on three sides with lush vineyards and orchards, and Lake Ontario on the fourth. And it is home to the famous Shaw Festival every summer. Visitors must wonder whether Niagara On The Lake perhaps got more than its share somehow.

## *"Push on, brave York Volunteers!"*

Sir Isaac Brock 1812
*Celebrated in story and song, the dying command of the leader of British and militia forces in the War of 1812, is recalled to this day. It was at the battle of Queenston Heights on October 13th, 1812 that the General fell to an American sniper's bullet moments after uttering his famous words. Sir Isaac Brock and Laura Secord, the nurse whose celebrated night-time trek to warn of an impending attack by the Americans, have emerged as the hero and heroine of the War of 1812. Canadians are fond of joking that; "If it weren't for this brave girl, we'd be eating Martha Washington's chocolates today".*

# Fort George

First headquarters for General Sir Isaac Brock at the beginning of the War of 1812, Fort George today is a beautifully restored example of a turn-of-the-century British fortification. The fort features eight authentically refurnished buildings, staff in period costume and demonstrations of 1812 music, musket and cannon fire, drill, blacksmithing, cooking and daily life.

## Niagara Wines

The Niagara Peninsula is the premier wine-growing region in Ontario. Grape vines have been planted here for 200 years, and the region accounts for over 80 per cent of the wine grapes grown in Canada. Many Niagara wines today take their place among the great wines of the world. Geography is key to the creation of fine wines and Ontario's vineyards are in a cool-climate growing season similar to that of Germany, Champagne and Burgundy. The Niagara region also benefits from a unique microclimate created by Lakes Erie and Ontario and the Niagara Escarpment, protecting the 7,000 hectares (18,000 acres) of vineyards throughout the coldest months.

*Konzelmann Estate Winery, Niagara On The Lake.*

*Vineyard on Jordan Bay near the appropriately named town of Vineland.*

*Greenhouse complex of Creekside Growers who produce seasonal plants including poinsettia and easter lilies under 250,000 square feet of glass.*

*Known locally as a replica of Columbus' ship, The Nina, this vessel began life as a floating casino near Cornwall, Ontario. Motorists speeding by must wonder what she is doing grounded in her little harbour.*

# Welland Canal

As part of the St. Lawrence Seaway, the Welland Canal, joining Lake Ontario and Lake Erie, is one of the world's great engineering triumphs. Built to circumvent nature's wonder, Niagara Falls, the canal provides a man-made deep waterway system for ocean vessels and lakers to navigate into the heart of the continent. The seven locks lift a ship 100 metres (326 feet), the difference in water levels between Lake Ontario and Lake Erie.

*Freighter 'Trias' entering Lock 3 during her descent through the Welland Canal to Lake Ontario. Locks 4, 5 and 6 can be seen in the background.*

*Tourists getting close-up look at locking operation. The Welland Canals Centre and St. Catharines Museum at bottom right offers interpretive and historical information.*

*This ship has reached the bottom of the lock; the door is open and she is about to sail out to the open Lake Ontario.*

*View up the Niagara River Gorge to the twin cascades in 1925. The town of Niagara Falls, New York is visible at left; while Niagara Falls, Ontario is on the right.*

*In 1927 we see a few more buildings and get a good view of the Rainbow Bridge spanning the Niagara Gorge.*

*"Nature will be Nature still, while palaces shall decay and fall in ruins Yes, Niagara will be Niagara a thousand years hence! The rainbow, a wreath over her brow, shall continue as long as the sun, and the flowing of the river – while the work of art, however impregnable, shall in atoms fall!"*

George Copeway, Objibwa spokesperson, 1860s.

# Niagara Falls

*In this dramatic, straight down view from above the Canadian, Horseshoe Falls, we get a misty view of Niagara Falls, Ontario in the distance. Photo: Russ Heinl*

# Orillia

Nestled between Lake Couchiching and Simcoe, Orillia is a fast-growing community with an historical downtown. Orillia is also the city that inspired Canada's premiere humourist, Stephen Leacock, to write "Sunshine Sketches of a Little Town".

*View of Orillia on Lake Couchiching.*

*Stephen Leacock National Historic Site at Orillia. Visitors can tour his home and the rebuilt boathouse where Leacock wrote each morning, have lunch or English tea at the Lake Wissanoti Terrace Café and visit the gift shop.*

*"Mariposa is not a real town. On the contrary, it is about seventy or eighty of them. You may find them all the way from Lake Superior to the sea, with the same square streets and the same maple trees and the same churches and hotels, everywhere the sunshine of the land of hope."*

Stephen Leacock 1912
*Leacock was frequently accused of modeling his fictional Mariposa on the Ontario town of Orillia, where he spent his summers in a residence that is now a museum dedicated to his life and work. But Mariposa was the quintessential small Ontario town of the time, populated with lovable eccentrics who were faced with "happy problems". This amusing defense against the charge appears as the preface to his classic work, Sunshine Sketches of a Little Town (1912).*

Pastoral farmland north of Orillia, bathed in soft light of late afternoon.

Is it possible that this farmer's last name begins with the letter 'S'?

*Muskoka Sands Resort on Lake Muskoka at Gravenhurst.*

*Port Carling between Lake Muskoka at bottom and Lake Rosseau.*

*Royal Muskoka Lodge, typical of the grand old resorts that thrived in this area for all of this century. This one, like many of its kind, was destroyed by fire 50 years ago.*

Visitors have been drawn for many years to the Muskoka Lakes – sparkling blue jewels sprinkled among the forest and set in the granite of the Cambrian Shield, with resorts and cottages nestling everywhere.

*Muskoka*

*Royal Mail Ship (RMS) Segwun steamship at her dock in Gravenhurst. North America's oldest operating steamship, built in 1887, offers daily cruises on the Muskoka Lakes.*

*Summer homes of southern Ontario's rich and famous are concentrated in the Muskoka Lakes district. Many have maintained their grand boathouses, like their marvelous old 'cottages', in fine style.*

# Georgian Bay

Immortalized by our famous Canadian painters, the Group Of Seven, Georgian Bay offers visitors the uniquely rugged splendor so characteristic of this area of Lake Huron. Imagine a weekend on an island like that pictured here, exploring the glacial striations in the photo at right by sea-kayak or paddling the hundreds of uninhabited, inland lakes like the ones pictured below, by canoe.

*"Canada. What a beautiful country. The air and the sky seem to have been freshly washed and polished, and the people too."*

Marlene Dietrich, movie star in the 1930s.

*"The girls are out to Bingo and
the boys are gettin' stink-o.
We think no more of Inco on a
Sudbury Saturday night."*

Stompin' Tom Connors, composer and performer,
first lines of "Sudbury Saturday Night", included
by Bob Davis in Singin' about Us (1976)

Inco's mining, milling, smelting and refining complex west of Sudbury in 1999. One
of the largest in the world, it produces nickel, copper and other metals as well as
chemicals for use by industry. In the photo at top right on the opposite page, we see
the International Nickel operation as it looked after its first 25 years of operation in
1928. This photo reflects a name change to Inco and a further 75 years of growth.

*Molten slag being dumped.*

*View of International Nickel Company's operation in 1928.*

# Sudbury

Following its humble beginnings in 1883 as a tiny railway settlement, the Sudbury area developed as a lumbering and agricultural community before becoming a world-renowned centre of mining excellence with the arrival of International Nickel in 1902. Geologists believe the mineral-rich Sudbury basin was formed 2 billion years ago when a huge meteorite struck.

Sudbury, serving half a million people in Northern Ontario, is a major centre for government, medical care, education and commercial services.

*"Once described as "Canada's Pittsburgh without the orchestra", Sudbury now has its own symphony…"*

Peter C. Newman, *columnist, Maclean's April 1st, 1991.*

*View of Sudbury's downtown and rail yards with Ramsey Lake in the foreground.*

# Thunder Bay

The city of Thunder Bay was born in 1970, the result of the amalgamation of Fort William and Port Arthur. But its roots go back a little further than that.

Thunder Bay's central location in the middle of a continent and at the head of the Great Lakes made it a natural meeting and trading site as far back as the Paleo-Indian civilization 11,000 years ago. Europeans arrived in the 17th century, establishing a series of fur trading outposts at the place they named Baie de Tonnerre, or Thunder Bay. In 1798, the North West Company built Fort William which quickly became a lively community of Scottish traders, French voyageurs and Native trappers. Prince Arthur's Landing, just a few miles to the east, had an excellent, natural harbour on Lake Superior.

But the die for today's Thunder Bay was cast in 1875 when the federal government designated it the Lake Superior terminus of the transcontinental railroad. "The Lakehead" was to become a major trans-shipment point for lumber and wheat. In 1884 the first terminal grain elevator was built in Fort William, and the first shipment of Manitoba wheat to eastern markets was made.

*"Long before one reaches it one sees the mountainous wheat elevators in which much of the western harvest is stored until it can be shipped eastwards. They have been called the "Castles of Commerce", and from a distance they look like a combination of the great keep of a Norman fortress, with the pillars of Luxor built into it. There is one which is alone sufficient to hold the bread-supply of the whole population of the United Kingdom for five days."*

Sir Arthur Conan Doyle, author and traveler, evoking the grain elevators at present-day Thunder Bay, Our Second American Adventure. (1923).

*View of the shoreline looking to the south with Mount McKay and the "Norwesters" in the background. Photo: Jeanette Lightwood*

National Air Photo Library / HA504.45

*View of a portion of the same shoreline as above, in 1927.*

*"I'm seventy-five. I would have been seventy-six, but I spent a year in Thunder Bay."*

Red Skelton, *comedian performing in Toronto, 1989.*

Two Views of the downtown "Port Arthur" area in 1999 and 1927 - bottom right. People familiar with Thunder Bay will recognize Prince Arthur's Landing and Marina Park. The CN Station, Armoury, Port Arthur Collegiate, Prince Arthur Hotel, the "Pagoda" and St. Paul's Trinity United and St. Andrew's Roman Catholic churches, all visible in both the contemporary photograph and the 1927 view at bottom right. Photo: Jeanette Lightwood

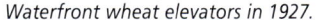

*Waterfront wheat elevators in 1927.*

(5-49) National Air Photo Library / HA504-46

*Waterfront wharfs in 1927.*

National Air Photo Library / HA504-48

129

*View of harbourfront area looking east. We see a portion of the lovely park on the shore of Lake of the Woods, the "MS Kenora" tour boat, Main Street and the float plane base.*

# Kenora

Originally called Rat Portage from an Indian word which means the "road to the country of the muskrat", the town became Kenora in 1905 when public pressure won out over sentimentalism. Even then the area was recognized as a tourist destination and how attractive would the name "Rat Portage" sound to potential visitors? There is also the story that a flour mill refused to build in the town because it objected to having the word "rat" appear on its bags.

From its beginnings as a Hudson's Bay Company fur trading post, Kenora developed into – for a time – the town with the roughest reputation in Canada. The resource-rich area drew a wide variety of pioneers and even led to a boundary dispute where, at one point, Kenora was claimed by both Manitoba and Ontario.

Ontario won, the ruffians drifted off and today, Kenora is a full service community on the north shore of Lake of the Woods that draws tourists from around the world.

*View of downtown area looking north up Main Street.*

Float plane base for Walsten Air, a living example of the famous Canadian legend, the "bush flying operator" specializing in flying sportsmen from all over the world into remote lakes reachable only by air.

# Lake of the Woods

The gem of Northwestern Ontario is surely Lake of the Woods, a massive body of water with 65,000 miles of shoreline surrounding an astounding 14,500 islands.

The lake, bounded by Ontario, Manitoba and Minnesota offers splendid fishing in addition to thousand year-old pictographs, forgotten gold mines and towering granite hills. Hikers and naturalists love the rocky cliffs and the abundant wildlife – hunters and anglers have their choice of lodges and outpost camps. And for sailors there's a seven-day race and cruise, the Lake of the Woods International Sailing Association Regatta, the largest inland regatta in North America.

According to one Cree legend, the lake was created by a Wendigo, one of their lesser gods. In a fit of whimsy he decided to create a lake spectacular in its uniqueness. He then congested the northern half of the lake with islands and water, creating a masterful maze of narrow channels, sheltered inlets and treacherous reefs. So enthralled was he with his creation that he transformed himself into a rock so he could forever marvel at his own handiwork.

A few of the 14,500 islands that inspired the name; Lake of the Woods.

# The Arctic

*"The north focuses our anxieties. turning to face north, we enter our own unconscious. Always, in retrospect, the journey north has the quality of dream."*

Margaret Atwood, *novelist, "True North", Saturday Night, January, 1987.*

Crystalline forest in the southern Yukon Territory. Photo: Hans Blohm

*"There is no authentic report of wolves ever having killed a human being in the Canadian North; although there must have been times when the temptation was well-nigh irresistible."*

Farley Mowat, *author and naturalist,*
Never Cry Wolf *(1963).*

Sea ice forming in Lancaster Sound, Ellesmere Island National Park, Nunavut. Photo: Hans Blohm

Adams Glacier, Ellesmere National Park, Nunavut. Photo: Parks Canada, Wayne Lynch / 12.122.03 07. (170)

St. Elias Mountains, Kluane National Park, Yukon Territory. Photo: Photo: Parks Canada / 11.110.03.07 (10)

# The Yukon

"A bunch of the boys
were whooping it up
in the Malamute saloon:
The kid that handles
the music-box was
hitting a rag-time tune;
Back of the bar,
in a solo game,
sat Dangerous
Dan McGrew,"

There are strange things done in the midnight sun
By the men who moil for gold;
The Arctic trails have their secret tales
That would make your blood run cold;
the Northern Lights have seen queer sights,
But the queerest they ever did see
Was that night on the marge of Lake Lebarge
I cremated Sam McGee."

Robert W. Service 1907
*These lines will be recognized as the opening verses of two of the most popular ballads of the twentieth century.*
*"The Shooting of Dan McGrew" and "The Cremation of Sam McGee" were composed by this Scots-born bank clerk*
*who came to be recognized as the Poet of the Yukon. They were published in his first collection, Songs of a Sourdough (1907)*

Backpacker's reaction to view of Lowell Glacier, Kluane National Park, Yukon Territory. Photo: Parks Canada / 11.110.09.07 (26)

Kluane National Park, Yukon Territory. Photo: Parks Canada, Wayne Lynch / 110.03.08 (74)

*"Lying flat on your back on Ellesmere Island on rolling tundra without animals, without human trace, you can feel the silence stretching all the way to Asia."*

Barry Lopez, naturalist, *Arctic Dreams: Imagination and Desire in a Northern Landscape* (1986).

Kaskawulsh Glacier with Mount Logan in background. Photo: Parks Canada, Wayne Lynch / 11.110.03.10 (594)

*"The Arctic is lifeless, except for millions of caribou and foxes, tens of thousands of wolves and musk oxen, thousands of polar bears, millions of birds, and billions of insects."*

Vilhjalmur Stefansson, Arctic explorer.

Mount Logan and Icefield Ranges, Kluane National Park, Yukon Territory. Photo: Parks Canada, Mike Beedell / 11.110.03.10 (304)

*"I have seen the Great Mackenzie Valley and the fantastic sight of the Mackenzie Delta, one hundred and fifty miles of wriggling channels and little ponds. I have seen it from the air at sunset. Somebody once described it as a giant mirror splintered into ten thousand pieces shining up to you."*

Pierre Berton, *author, address Empire Club of Canada, Toronto, October 11th, 1973.*

ESSO oil rigs at Norman Wells on the MacKenzie River. Photo: Hans Blohm

MacKenzie River Delta, North West Territories. Photo: Hans Blohm

*"The more I see of the country, the less I feel I know about it. There is a saying that after five years in the north every man is an expert; after ten years, a novice."*

Pierre Berton, author, The Mysterious North (1956, 1939).

*"Man enters the picture only as a small, insignificant figure, dwarfed by the immensity of the land. May the relationship always be so."*

Pat and Rosmarie Keough, *nature writers and photographers*, The Nahanni Portfolio *(1988)*

*Virginia Falls on the Nahanni River, Nahanni National Park, North West Territories. Photo: Parks Canada, Mike Beedel / 12.120.03.04 (15)*

Mountain range in Auyuittuq National Park, Nunavut, Baffin Island. Photo: Parks Canada / 12.121.03.10 (59)

*"And yet, there is only*
*One great thing,*
*The only thing:*
*To live to see, in huts and on journeys*
*The great day that dawns*
*And the light that fills the world."*

Eskimo Song 1921
*These evocative words come from "a little nameless Eskimo song" that*
*was sung by the Inuit at Kent Peninsula, N.W.T. and recorded by the*
*Danish-Eskimo explorer Knud Rasmussen on the Fifth Thule Expedition*
*in the Arctic, 1921-24; from the Mackenzie Eskimo (1942).*

*Peaks of the Unclimbables, Ragged Range, Nahanni National Park, North West*
*Territories. Photo: Parks Canada, Mia et Klaus / 12.120.03.10 (26)*

Port of Churchill under construction in 1930.

Early stages of construction at port of Churchill in 1929.

Ports Canada grain elevators in 1998.

# Churchill

The first Europeans to arrive in Churchill were not looking for new places to live, but for a Northwest Passage to the spice-rich Orient. Jens Munk, a Danish navigator, led an ill-fated expedition which wintered beside the Churchill River near its mouth in 1619-20. One hundred years later the Hudson's Bay Company established a trading post in the area. The massive Prince of Wales Fort was built in the latter part of the 18th Century.

Western Canadians' demand for a prairie port eventually brought about construction of the Hudson Bay Railroad and the Port of Churchill. The last spike of the railroad was driven in 1929 and the first two ships loaded with grain left the port in 1931.

During World War II the United States Air Force built Fort Churchill east of the town and, after the war, Canada and the United States jointly operated a training and experimental centre on the site. The base was officially closed in August of 1980. New rental housing and a large Town Centre were constructed in the 1970's as part of a redevelopment project financed by the Provincial and Federal Governments.

Prince of Wales' Fort, National Historic Site is situated on the west bank of the Churchill River. This massive fort was built during a 40-year period beginning in 1731.

*"Hudson's Bay is certainly a country that Sinbad the Sailor never saw, as he makes no mention of mosquitoes."*

David Thompson 1784
*This amusing observation was made by the geographer while resident at Prince of Wales' Fort in 1784–85.*

This freighter ran aground in the 1950s a few miles south of Churchill.

This WW II era, C-46 cargo plane crash landed about a mile from Churchill's runway. As with the ocean freighter above, there was no loss of life in these accidents.

143

*Lower Fort Garry National Historic Park, a short drive north along the Red River from Winnipeg, is the oldest stone fur-trading post still intact in North America. The fort also served as a staging and training base for the fledgling North West Mounted Police prior to their historic march west to bring law and order to that land in 1874.*

*"Come and sit by my side if you love me,*
*Do not hasten to bid me adieu*
*But remember the Red River Valley*
*And the girl who has loved you so true."*

*According to folklorist Edith Fowke, in Singing Our History (1984),*
*this perennially popular western folk song was probably composed*
*in Manitoba at the time of the Red River Rebellion of 1870.*
*Folk Song 1870*

*The romanesque St-Boniface Basilica, built in 1908, was destroyed by*
*fire in 1968 but remains as an elegant facade to the new structure,*
*built in 1972. It is located in the French Quarter of St. Boniface, home*
*to the largest French speaking community in western Canada.*

> *"Toronto people are just as sure Winnipeg is in the West as Vancouver people are that it is in the East."*
>
> Barry Mather, *journalist and one-time Parliamentarian.*

# Winnipeg

One of the best ways to see the growth of a community is from the air. The two 19th century views to the right show the population explosion that followed the arrival of the railway. In 1873, before the Canadian Pacific Railway came to town, the population was just 1,000. In 1880, the rails had arrived and the population jumped to 8,000. Then, in just four years the city on the Red River boasted nearly 40,000 souls. Look at the development on the finger-like peninsula in the foreground of all three aerial images.

Contemporary aerial view of Winnipeg.

*Bird's eye view of Winnipeg from 1884.*

*Bird's eye view of Winnipeg from 1880.*

# Winnipeg

If a community can be said to have a heart, Winnipeg's must surely beat at the confluence of the Red and Assiniboine Rivers. If we review our questionable custom of tracing the roots of our cities and towns to the arrival of the first Europeans – an increasingly relevant exercise – the archaeological evidence suggesting indigenous peoples first gathered here 6,000 years ago for trade and commerce, would give Winnipegers an interesting claim to being Canada's oldest city.

Modern Winnipeg traces its beginnings to 1738 when Pierre de La Verendrye established a fur trading post here. The settlement, known as the Red River Colony, was a hub for the fur trade until the 1880's when grain production became the principal industry in Western Canada. With completion of the trans-continental railroad, the newly incorporated city of Winnipeg became the "gateway to the West" and enjoyed a thirty-year growth boom. When the railway arrived in 1880 the city had a population of about 4000. Today 680,000 people enjoy Manitoba's capital city at the juncture of the Red and Assiniboine Rivers.

As the hub city within a large geographical region, Winnipeg boasts a dynamic cultural diversity. Relocating immigrant groups have brought together influences from around the world and contributed to the development of the city's unique districts.

*"It is a very nice place to live; there are no wars."*

*Unidentified Ukrainian farmer, then in his nineties, who lived close to Bird's Hill Park, near Winnipeg, quoted by Dian Cohen and Kristin Shannon in* The Next Canadian Economy *(1984).*

*The "Forks" on the Assiniboine River.*

# The Forks

Christened "The Forks" by European fur traders, the area was always a centre of commerce and transportation. But for most of the twentieth century it was devoted to the storage of railway cars and was anything but a people place. With the abandonment of the rail yards in the 1980's, the people returned and the Forks of today is Winnipeg's favourite public gathering place, virtually unrecognizable in its vibrant, modern form. Restaurants, shops, historic buildings, the Riverwalk, dock and the Forks National Historic Site all combine to charm locals and visitors alike.

> *"No man in Canadian history suffered as many reversals of fortune during his life. He was, in turn, unofficial leader of his people, president of a provisional government, founder of the Province of Manitoba, fugitive in exile, member of Parliament, outlaw, leader of another provisional government, and prisoner."*
>
> Pierre Elliot Trudeau, *Prime Minister's, address at the unveiling of the Louis Riel Monument, Regina, October 2nd, 1969*

*Legislative Building. This stately neo-classical structure, topped by the famous Golden Boy statue, rises from 12 hectares of manicured gardens.*

*National Air Photo Library / A949.21*

*View down Broadway, past the Legislative Building, toward the Hotel Fort Garry and the CN Station in 1928.*

*National Air Photo Library / A949.23*

*View of Hotel Fort Gary looking east towards the downtown area. The CN Station on Main Street is also visible, just a short block to the east. Opened in 1913, it is one of the hotels built by the railways early in the century in the uniquely Canadian Chateau style.*

*Hotel Fort Garry in 1998.*

*Portage & Main*

View of the Forks, Winnipeg's famous meeting place, where the Assiniboine joins the Red River. Main Street runs diagonally to the top of the photo for its meeting with Portage Avenue.

View north on Main Street towards Portage Avenue in 1928.

Without a doubt, the windiest corner in Canada, Portage and Main is today the business core of the city where bank and office towers dominate. The "old Portage Trail" arriving from all points west (now Portage Avenue and part of the Trans Canada Highway) used to end at this intersection. And those prairie winds that blow across 2000 km of flatland from the west have nothing to slow them down until they bump up against downtown Winnipeg, where they are often diverted in a rather tumultuous manner by the 30-story buildings at this famous intersection.

View east along Portage Avenue toward Main Street in 1928.

Portage and Main in 1998.

151

# Saskatchewan

*"There is nothing remarkable or distinguished in admiring Niagara Falls or the Banff mountains; they are obviously admirable things. But a space that has the delicacy of not being loud, of not being adorned, in fact of hardly being at all, requires a different inspection. It demands an effort of both patience and imagination, like the abstract geometric mandalas used as instruments of contemplation in tantric yoga. In this sense, the Prairies are our most generous landscape because they highlight or explain nothing and allow us, instead, an unconditional freedom."*

Alberto Manguel, *cultural commentator, "Prairie Zen", The Globe and Mail's Destinations Magazine, April 1988*

*Classic row of grain elevators alongside the railway in the town of Fillmore.*

*"I believe it will take a thousand years to develop a national style in Canada, but I do see a light in the west over a grain elevator."*

*The preservation of the best from the past and the promotion of a national style in architecture were the twin concerns of architectural writer Eric Arthur.*
*Eric Arthur 1929*

*Farmer cutting his grain and creating wind rows for the combine which will come later, separating the kernels of grain from the chaff. The green, uncultivated land to the right is either too hilly or the earth is unsuitable for farming, so it is fenced off and used to graze cattle.*

Regina

"Regina rises from the
prairies of Saskatchewan
with a minimum of fuss."

Priit J. Vesilind, *writer*, "Common Ground, Different
Dreams", National Geographic, March 1990.

*Saskatchewan Legislative Assembly Building.*

In 1882, a tent settlement named Pile O' Bones sat on a treeless plain near a small, winding creek. The community that sprang from this humble beginning to become the capital of the province of Saskatchewan, is truly a testament to what can be accomplished with a vision, hard work, and a name change.

Regina's "emerald jewel," Wascana Centre, provides natural beauty and an escape from highrises and residential areas without leaving the city. One of the largest urban parks in North America, it is also the site of numerous cultural and historical attractions, and is home to the campuses of both the University of Regina and the Saskatchewan Provincial Legislative Building.

*View of Regina looking to the north over the area known as Wascana Centre, towards the downtown core. Saskatchewan's Legislative Assembly Building can be seen in its beautiful, lake-side setting.*

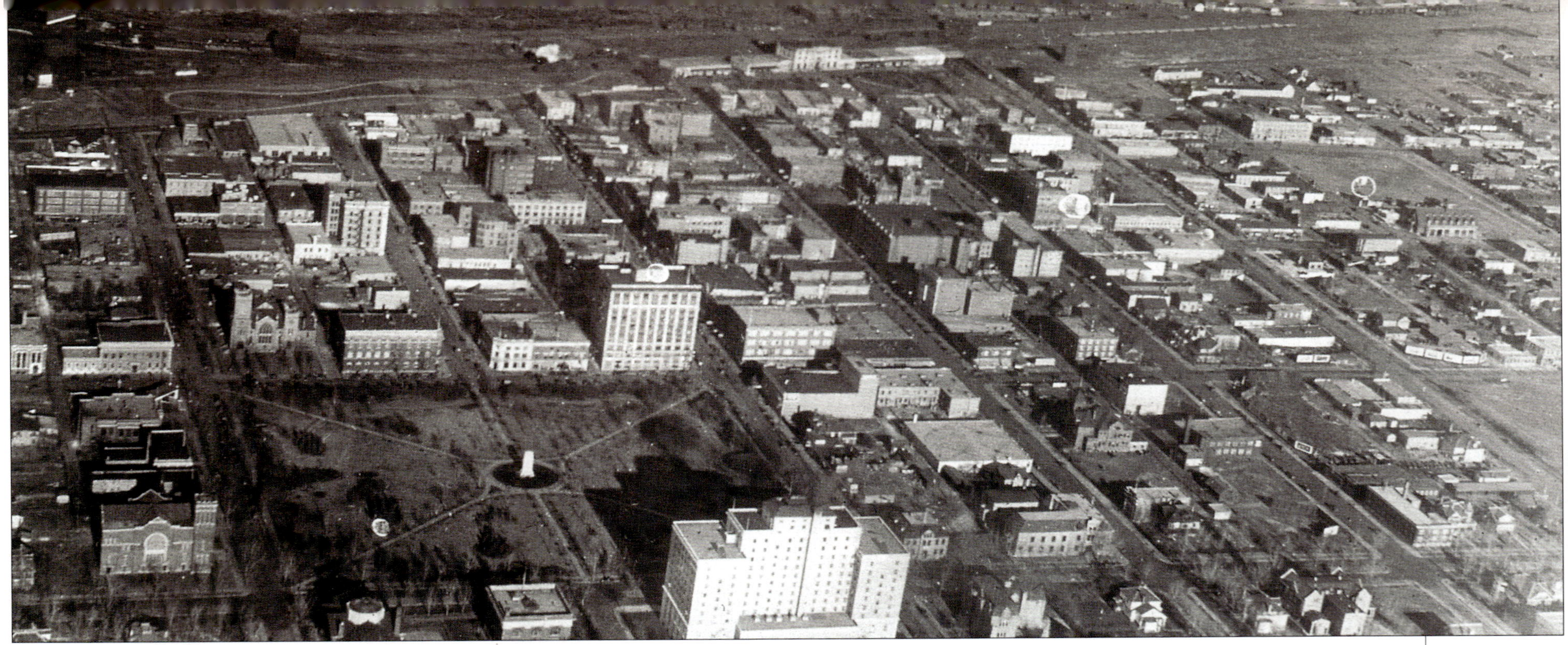

Saskatchewan Archives Board / RPL-B-331

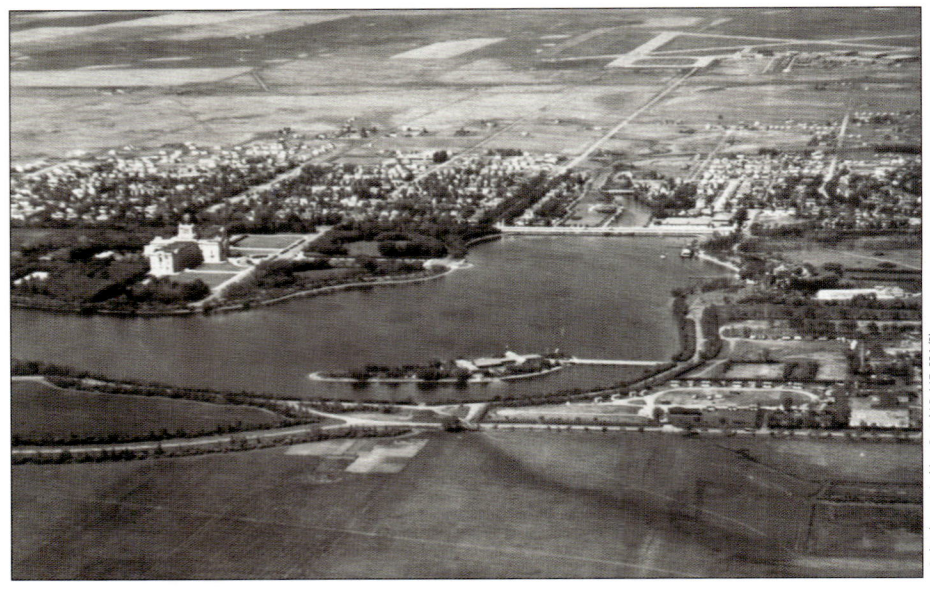

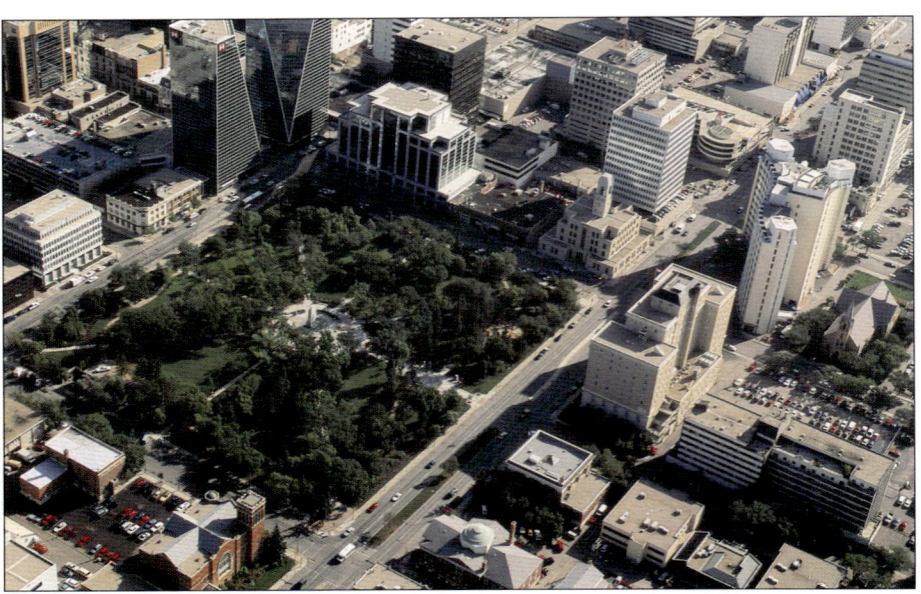

*Victoria Park, with another of those grand old railway hotels, the Hotel Saskatchewan is visible just below the park. In the colour photo below we see the same park in 1998 but the hotel is now the Hotel Saskatchewan Radisson Plaza. And the photo at bottom left is a view to the west over Wascana Lake to the airport.*

Saskatchewan Archives Board / R-A17, 824 (3)

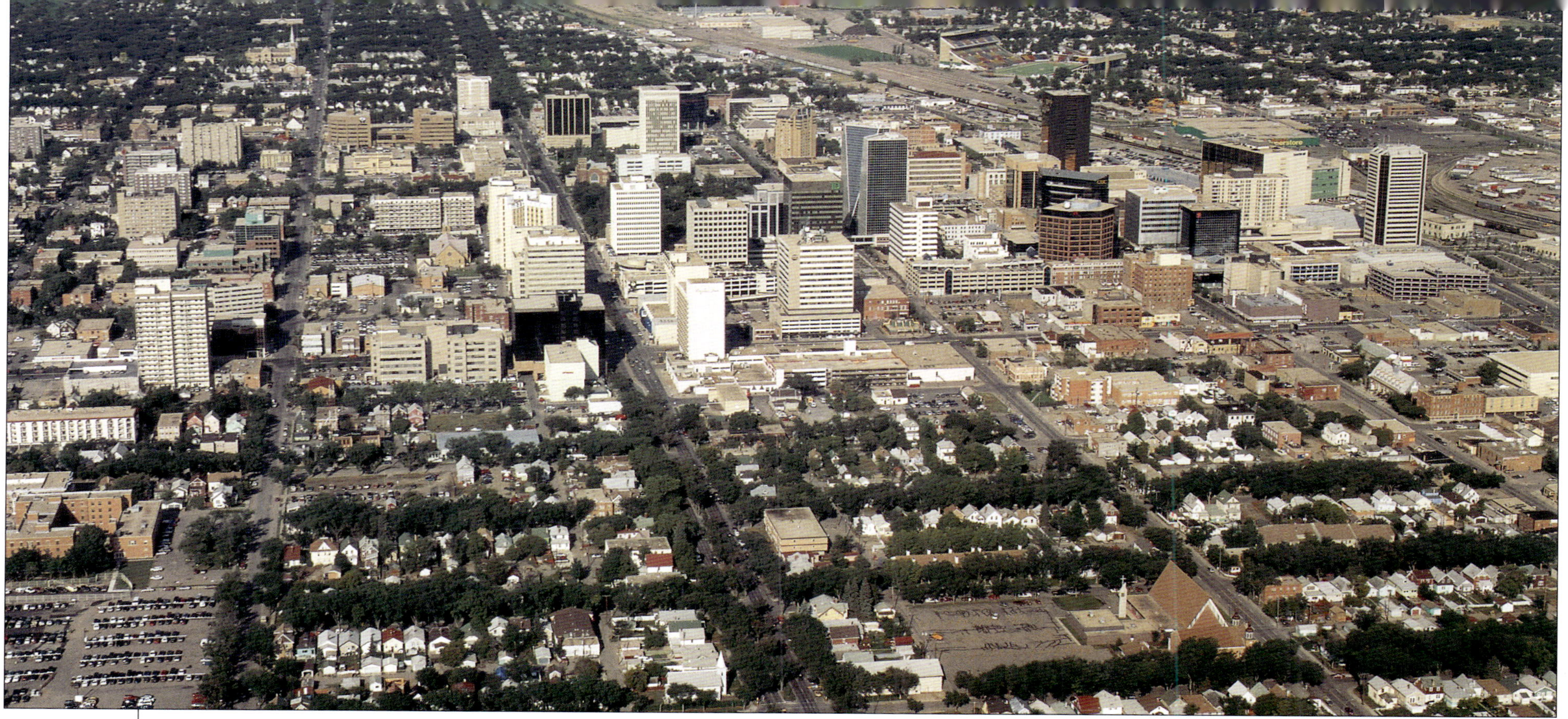

View looking over downtown to the west with the railway and Trans Canada Highway fading off over the horizon. The two colour photos below show Taylor Field, home of the CFL's Regina Roughriders, and the RCMP Training Academy, known simply as the Depot. The middle photo is a similar view to the contemporary image above but c. 1930

Saskatchewan Archives Board / R-A17, 421 (1)

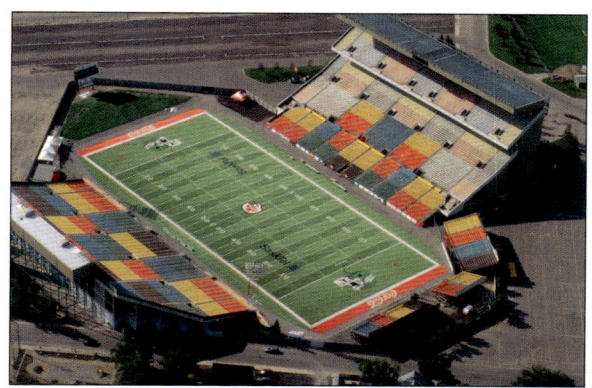

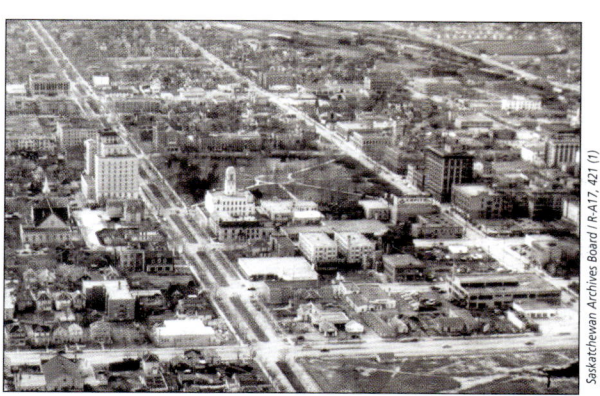

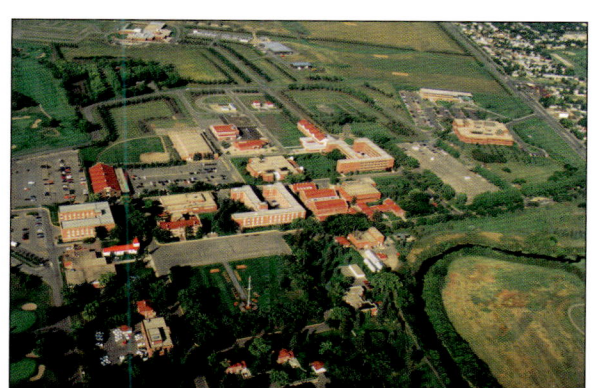

*Is this island in a sea of summer fallow near Fillmore, one farmer's proud salute to the homesteading couple at the top of the Canadian side of his family tree? Yes would be a good bet!*

Grasslands National Park in southern Saskatchewan.

"I am the grassland. Out of the abyss of a million years I have emerged. I have been a sea and a tropical jungle, the home of coral and the dinosaur. I have been a sleeping giant under the masses of glacial ice and I have awakened. I am a part of a changing earth, but for centuries my constancy has been my silence."

Opening paragraph of a poetically written brief submitted by Thelma Poirier, Killdeer, May 13th, 1976, Report of the Public Hearings Board on the Proposed Grasslands National Park issued by the Saskatchewan Ministry of Tourism, 1976.

Typical farm surrounded by wheat the family will turn into cash for the banker.

River View Huterite Colony on the South Saskatchewan River.

Truck leaving a prairie rooster tail in his wake.

159

*View of Saskatoon looking west over South Saskatchewan River towards the city center on the opposite shore.*

# *Saskatoon*

Saskatchewan's largest city is defined by the beautiful South Saskatchewan River that meanders through its heart. Originally a gathering place for early settlers, Saskatoon today is a university town, agricultural service centre, and base for mining, manufacturing and a flourishing high tech industry.

*View north to city-centre at left. The tiny section of bridge in the bottom, left corner is the bridge appearing on the opposite page. The modern, arched bridge in the contemporary photo will be built from the end of the wide road we see leading up to the river from the bottom of the old photo at left.*

The city was started as a Temperance Colony by John Lake in 1882. He wanted to call the settlement Minnetonka, but changed his mind after sampling "minaskwatomin", the purple berries that grew along the river. The Saskatoon of today is a far cry from what Lake and his teatotalling colonists envisioned in those early days, containing only the odd street named Temperance or Clearwater. But the berries that intrigued him remain, and a slice of Saskatoon Pie tempts many visitor's tastebuds.

*"Harvest: Annual ritual in which billions of dollars worth of machinery collects millions of dollars worth of wheat."*

"Pass for a Native: Learn These Terms", The Easterners' Guide to Western Canada (1965), edited by Ron Marken

The wonderful geometry of the wheat harvest on the Saskatchewan prairie

*"In the winter the beauty is even stronger. The Prairies eliminate the obviousness of a horizon and leave the traveler with the magnificence of an infinite blank page, land blending with sky. I have never understood "snow" to be a derogatory term."*

Alberto Manguel, *editor and writer, "Prairie Zen", The Globe and Mail's Destinations Magazine, April 1988.*

*Lone truck eastbound at sunrise on the Trans Canada Highway near Maple Creek.*

*Athabaska Glacier descending from the Columbia Icefields east, towards the Icefields Parkway, almost halfway between the Town of Jasper and the Village of Lake Louise. The building at bottom right is Parks Canada's Icefield Centre, where visitors can get interpretive information and arrange for a variety of tours. The Columbia Icefields' 150 square miles of snow is a "triple watershed" in that it's melt waters flow to the Atlantic, Pacific and Arctic Oceans. But snowflakes that fall here have to be patient because their glacial journey down to melting temperatures will take 10,000 years or so.*

# Alberta

*"In token of the love which thou hast shown*
*For this wide land of freedom, I have named*
*A province vast, and for its beauty famed,*
*By thy dear name to be hereafter known.*
*Alberta shall it be!"*

These are the first four lines of the fourteen-line verse
d'occasion composed by the Governor General on the subject of
why he had chose the name Alberta for the former District of
Assiniboia in 1882. Lorne named "a province vast" after his wife,
Louise Caroline Alberta, fourth daughter of Queen Victoria.
Marquis of Lorne 1882

Mount Assiniboine's Indian Peak in Mount Assiniboine Provincial Park. The border between Alberta
and British Columbia runs right up the ridge line in the foreground where the light on the Alberta
side meets the shadow of British Columbia.

"After Ottawa we went to the Rockies, to Lake Louise and Banff. Lake Louise was for a long time my answer when I was asked which was the most beautiful place I had ever seen: - a great long, blue lake, low mountains on either side, all of a most glorious shape, closing in with snow mountains at the end of it."

Agatha Christie, *mystery writer, stopping off at Banff and Lake Louise on a round-the-world trip made in 1922.* An Autobiography (1977)

A contemporary view of the resort and a 1924 view showing the hotel under construction.

*View of Lake Louise from the top of the valley.  Lake Louise is the small, aqua-marine jewel near the top of the large photo.*

*"A little while and I will be gone from among you, whither I cannot tell. From nowhere we came, into nowhere we go. What is life? It is a flash of a firefly in the night. It is a breath of a buffalo in the winter time. It is as the little shadow that runs across the grass and loses itself in the sunset."*

CROWFOOT, *Chief of the Blackfoot Indians, dying words, Blackfoot Crossing, Bow River, Alberta.*

*Badlands east of Drumheller. This image reflects perfectly Alberta's agriculture and oil based economy, and how they mix. Farmers and ranchers often sell oil companies rights to drill exploratory wells on their land. If oil or natural gas is found, a lease is negotiated and the ranch or farm will receive a supplementary income for as long as the well produces. Just such a producing well can be seen at the top of the plateau in the foreground.*

# Dinosaurs, Geology, and Oil

Many millions of years ago much of Alberta was part of a huge sea. During the dinosaur era, this area was warm, and hosted not only dinosaurs but generous vegetation needed to support such huge animals. Over millions of years this vegetation died and settled on the bottom of this sea. As continents shifted, Alberta became part of North America and the sediments were lifted well above sea level. The pressure of deep layers of rock on the decaying vegetation created the vast oil & gas reserves in Alberta today.

## Leduc #1

On a cold February day in 1947, news of a huge oil strike in Alberta was transmitted around the world. Residents from around the countryside and government officials gathered to watch as Vern "Dry Hole" Hunter and his crew from Imperial Oil hit the crude at 4:00 p.m.

Discovery at Leduc #1 signaled the start of a new era for Alberta and Canada. It proved to be the largest oil field tapped, to date, in Canada, diversifying Alberta's agriculture base. Four hundred and eighty million barrels of crude were eventually proven in this field.

### "Lord, Please Send Me Another Oil Boom and I Promise I Won't Piss It Away."

*Message on a bumper-sticker noted in Calgary, December, 1987.*

*Oil drilling crew at work in the Badlands east of Drumheller. The producing well at top of photo is the same one visible in the image on the opposite page.*

*The Canadian Petroleum Interpretive Centre & Hall of Fame and replica of Leduc #1. Raising a replica of the original derrick took place during the summer of 1990. The oil bearing Devonian Strata is 5,135 feet below where this commemorative rig now stands.*

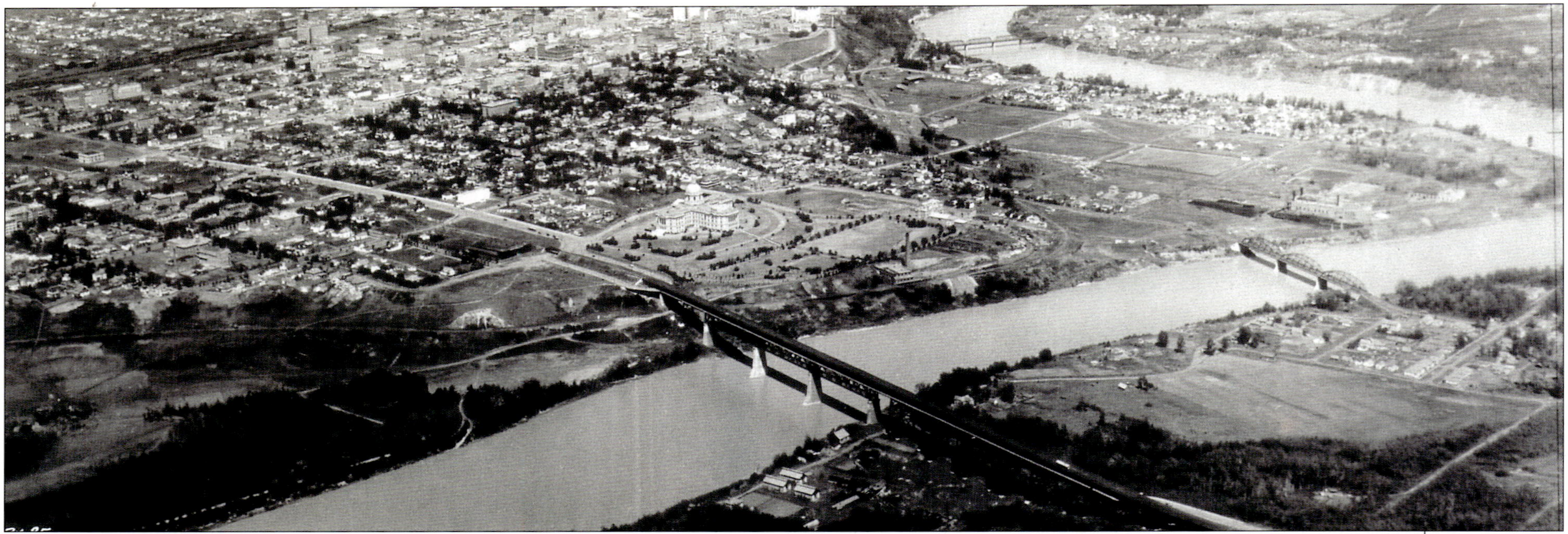

National Air Photo Library / CA124.85

*View eastwards over the North Saskatchewan River to the downtown core of Edmonton in 1925. The only prominent landmarks common to both these images are the Legislature of Alberta Building and the High Level and Walterdale Bridge just to the right.*

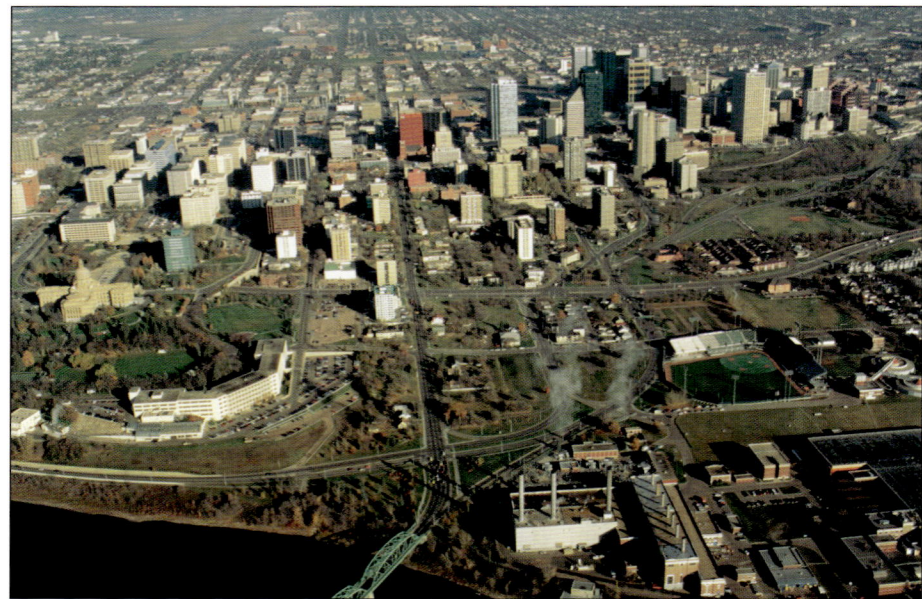

*View north over the North Saskatchewan River to the downtown core in 1998.*

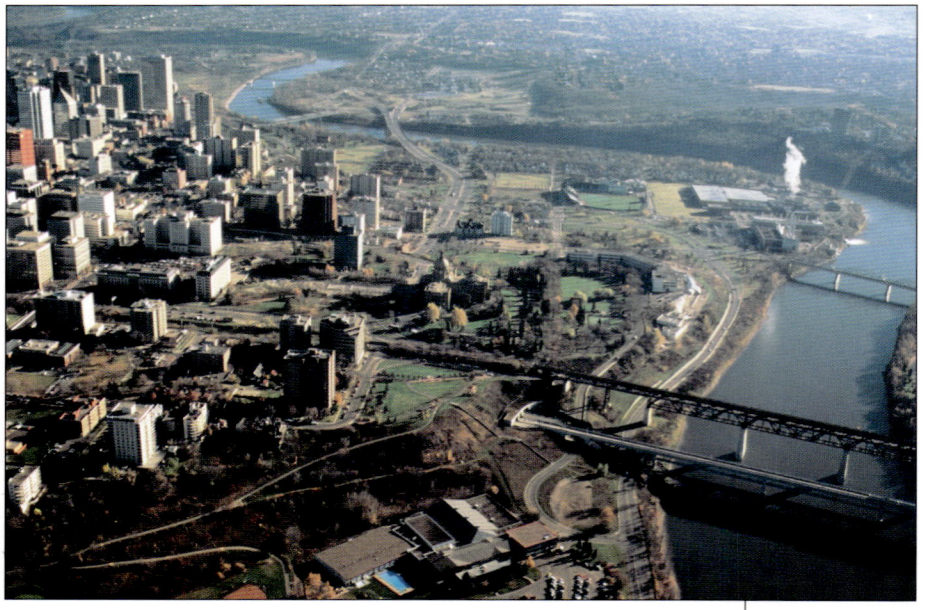

*View to the east showing the downtown area with the Legislature and the same two bridges; the High Level and the Walterdale. The LRT bridge is a relatively new addition.*

*West Edmonton Mall. The world's largest indoor shopping and entertainment complex has it all. A world class hotel, over 800 stores and services, 19 movie theaters, over 100 restaurants, Dolphin Presentations, Skating Rink, Galaxyland Amusement Park and the World Waterpark.*

*Alberta's Legislative Building.*

# Edmonton

Alberta's capital city, gateway to the north, and a major city of 625,000, is located on the banks of the North Saskatchewan River – once the original fur-trading route to the west.

Known the world over as the home of the spectacular West Edmonton Mall, Edmonton is a popular tourist destination offering outstanding museums, art galleries, and historical attractions. The City takes pride in its lush parks system, whose trails and walkways stretch out along the beautiful North Saskatchewan River Valley as it winds through the city.

*A fine example of the "railway Chateau", Canadian Pacific's Hotel MacDonald, an Edmonton landmark since 1915.*

A pair of CF-18 Hornets bank over Cold Lake in preparation for landing at Canadian Forces Base, Cold Lake.

## The Cowboy

The spirit of the west is alive and well in the rodeo arena and on the open range. The sport originated in the Old West where working cowboys competed with one another in events designed to show off their unique blend of skills. While the days when cattle ruled the prairie have faded, the sport of rodeo has continued to grow, and today there are thousands of rodeos staged every year. And there are still hundreds of working cattle ranches where cowboys tend to the herd from the back of a horse.

*Summer storm approaching prairie farmland near High River from the foothills of the distant Rocky Mountains.*

*There is nothing like a rodeo for good old, industrial strength, western entertainment and this one in High River is a perfect example.*

*Opening ceremonies underway at High River Rodeo.*

Participants in the Western Stock Growers' Great Centennial Cattle Drive push a herd of longhorn steers over the prairie to Medicine Hat in celebration of the organization's 100th anniversary.

Participants in the Great Centennial Cattle Drive following the chuck wagon.

Working cowboys finishing weaning calves from their mother cows at the OH Ranch near Longview.

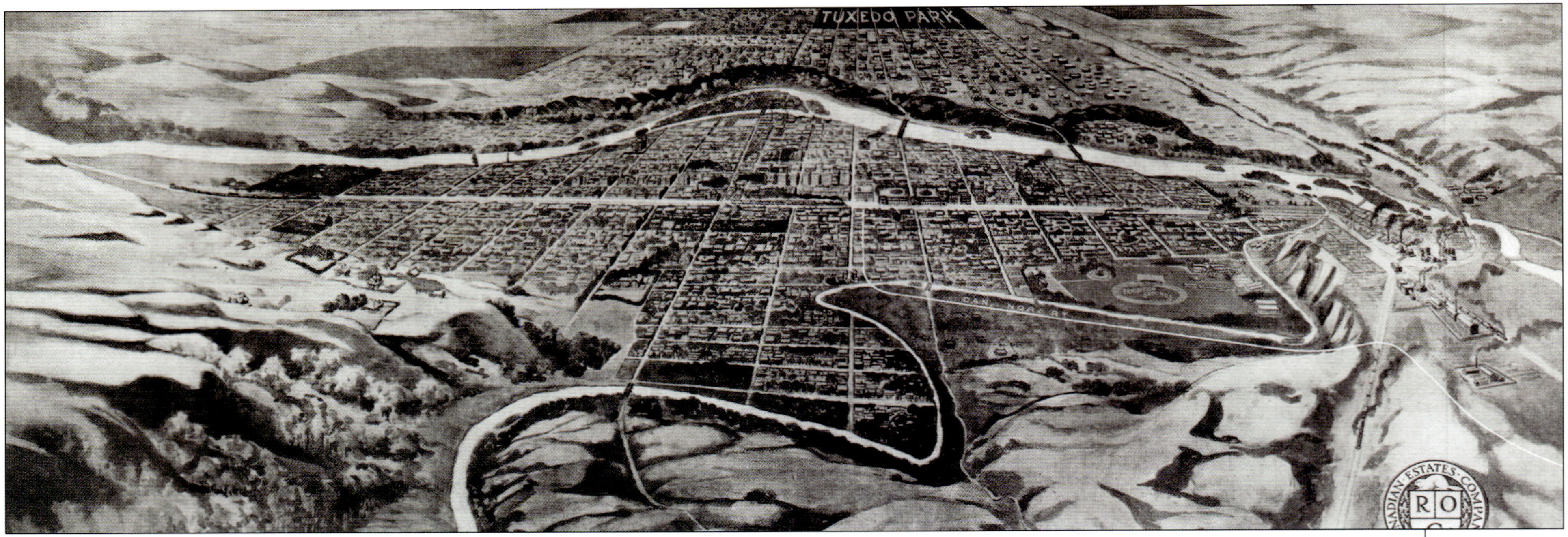


National Archives of Canada / NMC0043292

Bird's eye view of Calgary looking north to downtown and the Bow River in the very early 1900s.

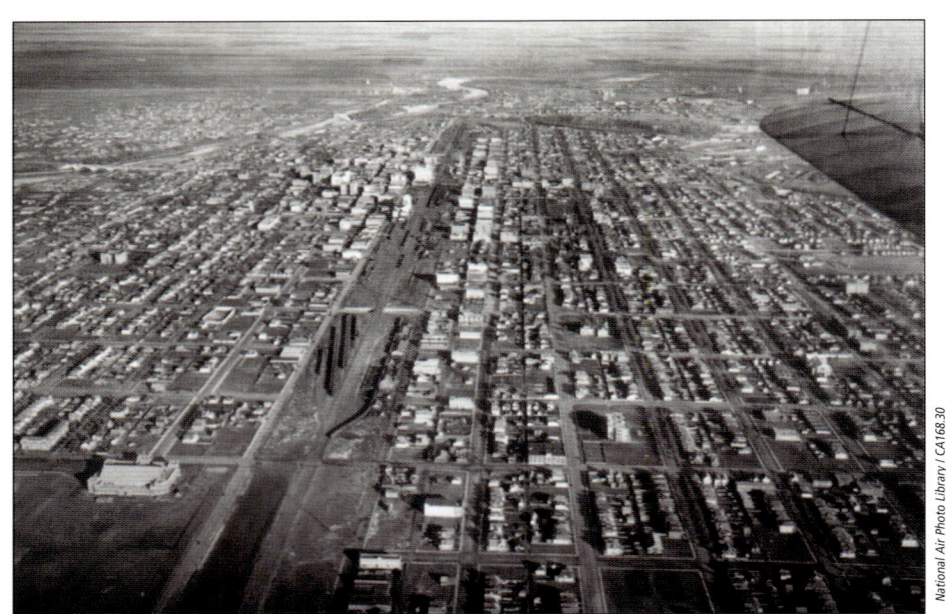

National Air Photo Library / CA168.30

*View of downtown core (and Royal Canadian Air Force biplane's wing tip) looking east along the railway main line in 1925.*

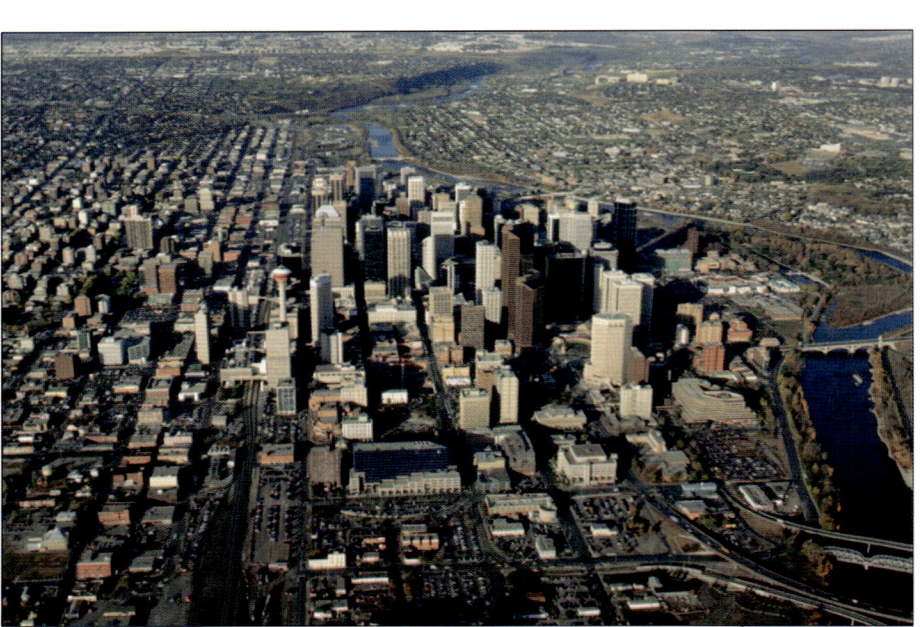

*View of downtown core looking west along the railway main line in 1998. The architectural evidence of several oil booms is very much in evidence.*

# Calgary

Located on the banks of the Bow River in the foothills of Alberta, this city of 820,000, with its spectacular Rocky Mountain backdrop to the west and the great plains to the east, offers the best of both worlds. A clean, safe, big city environment with all the amenities and an unspoiled mountain playground just an hour's drive away. Nowhere is this more evident than from the top of the landmark Calgary Tower. Looking west on a clear day people feel they can almost touch the majestic mountains while to the east the vast prairie stretches for 1300 kilometers, all the way to Winnipeg.

But like it or not, it is the Calgary Stampede for which this most western of cities is known around the world. For ten days in July everyone is a cowboy or cowgirl as the largest outdoor rodeo on earth turns the city into one big party. Apart from the wild west action in the rodeo arena, visitors get into the fun with pancake breakfasts on the streets, western dance parties, parades and an enormous midway and exhibition.

**The White Hatter Pledge of the Calgary Stampede.**
*"We, havin' pleasured ourselves considerable in the only genuine cowtown in Canada, namely Calgary, and havin' bin duly exposed to exceptional amounts of heartwarmin' tongue-loosin', back-slappin', neighbour-lovin' Western spirit; solemnly promise to communicate this here Calgary brand hospitality to all folks and critters who cross our trail thereafter."*

*Office towers in the downtown business district.*

*View looking to the west over the Calgary Exhibition and Stampede Grounds to the downtown core.*

*Just south of Lake Louise, in Banff National Park, lies Moraine Lake, in the shadow of the Valley of the Ten Peaks. For years it graced the back of the Canadian twenty-dollar bill, replaced a few years ago by another Canadian icon, the Loon, when the new "20" was introduced. Photo: Russ Heinl*

*Located in Yoho National Park, Takakkaw Falls, the second highest in Canada, means "magnificent" in the language of the Stoney Indians. Photo: Russ Heinl*

*Albertans familiar with the Rockies would be hard pressed to suggest any lake more deserving of the title; "most beautiful lake in the Rockies", than Lake O'Hara, in its magnificent, amphitheatre setting. Photo: Russ Heinl*

*"Morning Majesty"* is the title given to this image by the photographer, and it fits.  Sunburst Lake, and a mountain of the same name, dominate the foreground while Mount Assiniboine, tallest peak in the southern Rockies at 3,610 metres (11,840 feet), can be seen in the distance.  And if you were standing on Indian Peak, at Assiniboine's summit, you would have one foot in Alberta and the other in British Columbia. Photo: Bela Baliko

*British Columbia*

*"British Columbia is a large body of land entirely surrounded by envy."*

Eric Nichol, *humorist and one of the Vancouverite's favourite aphorisms.*

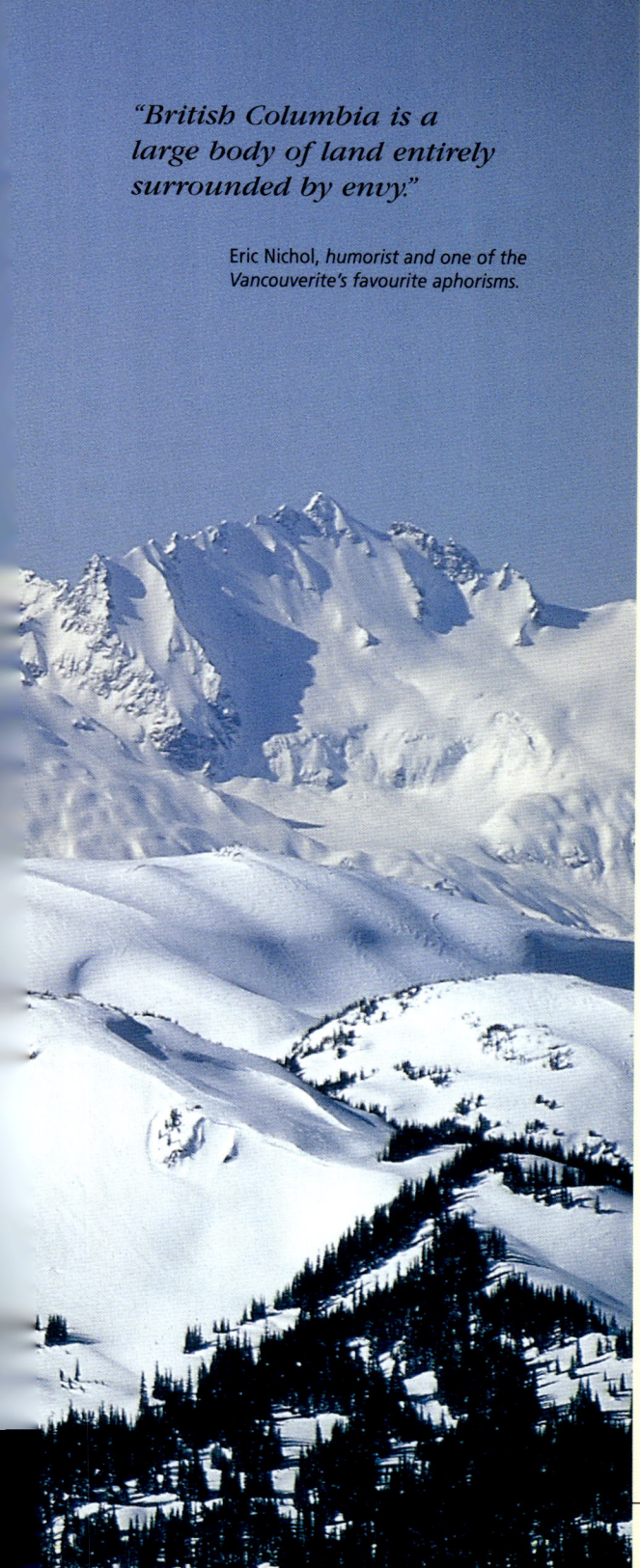

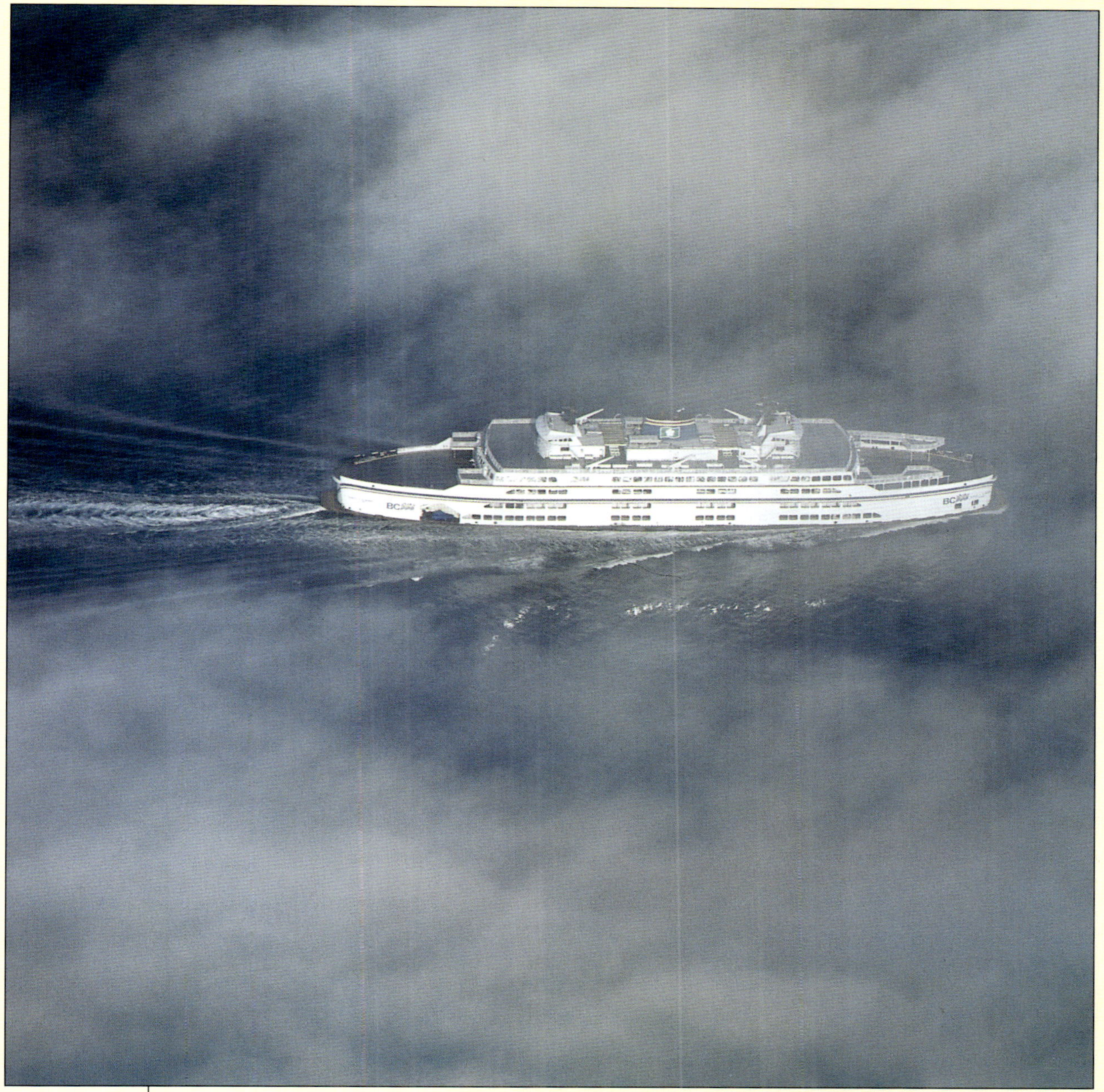

*BC Ferries' "Queen of Albernie" making her way through the mist shrouded waters in the Strait of Georgia, on her way from Nanaimo on Vancouver Island to Horseshoe Bay, just north of Vancouver.*

*View from over Whistler Mountain to Black Tusk and Tauntalus peaks in the Coastal Range. Photo: Chris Cheadle*

*Group of helicopter skiers waiting their turn for a flight to some remote mountain top near Whistler. Photo: Whistler Heli-Skiing Limited*

Group of heliskiers carving their way through virgin powder as their helicopter heads back down to lift another group up to their own unspoiled piece of mountain. Photo: Whistler Heli-Skiing Limited

*View north over beautiful Okanagan Lake to the city of Kelowna.*

# Kelowna

Situated on the shores of Lake Okanagan in the heart of wine country, over one million visitors annually are drawn to this lovely city with its lake and mountain setting. Many of them come back to stay. For Kelowna is fast becoming a retirement mecca and the 18 golf courses located within the city limits reflect this trend.

*View of downtown Kelowna with its Waterfront Park and marina.*

# Okanagan Valley

Located in central British Columbia, the largest and oldest wine-producing region is the Okanagan Valley. Today, there are over 30 wineries spread throughout the valley with a total of 3,000 acres of premium grape varieties. The south end of the valley gets less than six inches of rainfall a year, making it the only area in Canada to be classified as desert, while the north end of the valley receives less than sixteen inches. Classic red vinifera grapes are widely planted in the south end, while French and Germanic white grape varieties favour the northern climate.

*Vineyards perched on lake-side cliffs just south of Kelowna.*

*Gray Monk Estate Winery in Kelowna.*

*Wilderness park offering secluded hiking, camping and weekend anchorages within a few miles of downtown Kelowna.*

SEAT MUST BE IN
FORWARD 10 INCHES OF TRAVEL
DURING TAKEOFF AND LANDING

*"A sense of wonder is in itself a religious feeling. But in so many
people the sense of wonder gets lost. It gets scarred over. It's as
though a tortoise shell has grown over it. People reach a stage where
they're never surprised, never delighted. They're never suddenly
aware of glorious freedom or splendour in their lives. However hard
a life may be, I think for virtually all people this is possible."*

Robertson Davies, *man-of-letters, interviewed by Alan Twigg in* Strong Voices:
Conversations with Fifty Canadian Authors *(1988).*

*Looking down at Vancouver Airport through a wisp of British Columbia mist.*

Commercial air travel today is arguably the safest form of transportation available to us. Because of this high level of safety and the high altitudes aircraft operate at, we passengers come to take flying for granted, concentrating on the movie, our books, the food and drink. In the process, the elemental thrill of flying is lost and many people hardly bother to look out the window. So the next time you find yourself on a flight, ask the flight attendant if it would be possible to visit the cockpit. Most crews will welcome you up front and will appreciate your interest.

*Canadian Airlines, Boeing 747-400 cockpit as pilots line up for their final approach to Vancouver Airport. Captain Ted Prinsen has the left seat for this landing while First Officer Phil Tweten is handling radio communications and the checklists.*

189

# Vancouver

*To describe the beauties of this region will, on some future occasion, be a very grateful task to the pen of a skilled panegyrist. The serenity of the climate, the innumerable pleasing landscapes, and the abundant fertility that unassisted nature puts forth, requires only to be enriched by the industry of man with villages, mansions, cottages, and other buildings to render it the most lovely country that can be imagined; whilst the labour of the inhabitants would be amply rewarded, in the bounties which nature seems ready to bestow on cultivation.*

George Vancouver   1792

*Bird's eye view of downtown Vancouver looking south in 1898, from the site of present-day North Vancouver. The bustling harbour activity in Burrard Inlet reflects the change from sail to steam is already well underway as Vancouverites anticipate their approaching millennium.*

*View of Vancouver looking to the east, over Lost Lagoon in Stanley Park. This side-on view of Vancouver's port area shows the same waterfront depicted in the illustration on the opposite page.*

*Similar view of Vancouver to the one at left, but this is in 1925, only 28 years after the illustration on the opposite page.*

# *Vancouver*

The real beauty of Vancouver doesn't lie in its snowcapped peaks. Or its sandy beaches stretched along miles of shoreline. Or even in its lush, green forests and stunning floral displays. What makes Vancouver truly remarkable is that all this natural magnificence is more than matched by its man-made attractions. Sophisticated bistros, restaurants and outdoor cafes. Unique shops on cosmopolitan Robson, West Fourth and Granville Island. An architectural sensitivity has resulted in a downtown core that resonates with beautiful new buildings. From art galleries and museums to the vibrant theatre district and club scene, Vancouver is missing nothing.

Vancouver's real treasure is Stanley Park. Hidden amidst a paradise of giant cedars a visitor will discover miles of secluded trails along with unique garden displays, totems, an aquarium, miniature railway, petting zoo, tennis, lawn bowling, cricket, beaches, pitch-and-putt golf and her beautiful sea wall, another of our signature series of "Canadian Walks".

*Here we have a close-up view of Georgia Street approaching the causeway leading to Stanley Park, as it looked in 1925. Compare this same causeway area in the colour photo at left.*

In the foreground of this northward-looking view we see part of Kitsilano on the left, the Burrard and Granville bridges over False Creek, Vancouver's business core and her beautiful west end stretching around English Bay to Stanley Park at left. North Vancouver is visible on the horizon.

*View across Kitsilano Beach and English Bay to Vancouver's west end in 1925. The scrub in the foreground is now Vanier Park and the Kitsilano neighbourhood visible in the large colour photo.*

*Sun bathers and swimmers enjoying the beach on English Bay at the foot of Denman Street in 1925.*

*Astute Vancouverites will recognize Thurlow and Burrard Streets meeting Pacific Avenue at the east end of Sunset Beach on English Bay in 1925.*

*Lion's Gate Bridge connecting Vancouver's Stanley Park at right to the north shore.*

*BC Ferries terminal at Tsawwassen, south of Vancouver.*

*"Spirit of Vancouver Island" steaming across the Strait of Georgia from Victoria to Vancouver.*

*"We may paddle many moons on the sea, but our canoes will never enter the channel that leads to the yesterdays of the Indian people."*

Joe Capilano 1911
*This is the lament of the Squamish chief who recounted his people's tales and traditions to the poet Pauline Johnson, who published them in her book* Legends of Vancouver *(1911)*

*Ferries in Active Pass between Galiano and Mayne Islands, enroute between Victoria and Vancouver. Photo: Chris Cheadle*

Log booms anchored in a bay on the south-west coast of Vancouver Island near Victoria.

*Pulp and paper mill near Crofton on Vancouver Island.*

Bird's eye view of Victoria from over the Pacific Ocean in 1889.

British Columbia Archives / PDP04463

"To realize Victoria, you must take all that the eye admires in Bournemouth, Torquay, the Isle Of Wight, the happy valley at Hong Kong, the Doon, Sorrento, and Camp's Bay – add reminiscences of the Thousand Islands and arrange the whole around the Bay of Naples with some Himalayas for background."

Rudyard Kipling

Similar view in 1928.

Natinal Air Photo Library / A29.87

*View of Victoria looking north west from over the Pacific.*

# Victoria

Victoria has been charming visitors since before Kipling's time and it's easy to see why! The city is a jewel set in the midst of some of the most spectacular beauty in the world. It's no surprise to locals that Condé Nast Traveler Magazine's readers' poll rated Victoria one of the top ten cities to visit in the world. And, aside from all its charm, Victoria enjoys the mildest climate in Canada.

Victoria, the capital of British Columbia, was originally established by the Hudson's Bay Company in 1843 as a British fur trading post, and many of the beautiful character buildings throughout the city and especially downtown date back to the city's earliest years.

*View of Victoria looking north west from over the Pacific.*

National Air Photo Library / BA51.3

*Close up view of inner harbour in 1923.*

National Air Photo Library / A229.97

*Wide view of inner harbour and downtown in 1928.*

201

# Canada's West Coast Navy

Like their counterparts at HMC Dockyard in Halifax, Canadian sailors based in Esquimault range the Pacific in pursuit of Canada's defense interests throughout the Pacific Rim.

*View of Royal Canadian Navy base at Esquimault in 1928.*

View of dockyard facilities at HMC Dockyard, Esquimault in 1998

View of HMC Dockyard, Esquimault looking out through the harbour entrance to the Pacific in 1998.

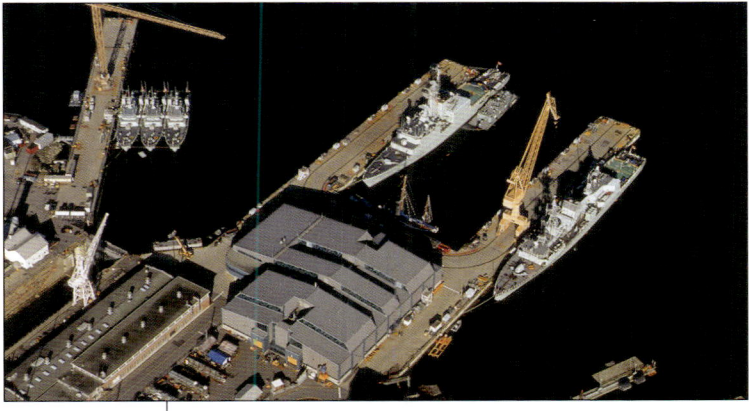

Close up view of dock area with several classes of navy vessels alongside.

An officer of the Canadian Navy stands at the fantail of a Canadian warship.

*"This is the flag of the future, but it does not dishonour the past."*

Lester B. Pearson 1964
*These words come from the speech delivered by the Prime Minister in the House of Commons "on December 15th. 1964, when Canada acquired its own distinctive flag, the Maple Leaf flag "to replace the Union Jack of Great Britain.*

CP-140 Aurora, maritime patrol aircraft of the Canadian Air Force over the Pacific.

Located on the west coast of Vancouver Island, near the famous Pacific Rim National Park, Tofino offers vacationers beach combing, biking, bird watching, hiking, diving, swimming, surfing, whale watching and sea kayaking. Photo: Chris Cheadle

Beachcombers searching the tidal flats of Rathtower Beach at Parksville. Photo: Chris Cheadle

*"The past is still, for us, a place that is not yet safely settled."*

Michael Ondaatje, *editor, Preface, The Faber Book of Contemporary Canadian Stories (1990).*

Combers ending their journey across the Pacific on beautiful, Long Beach near Tofino. Photo: Chris Cheadle

View of Campbell River looking north up to Discovery Passage. Internationally known as the "Salmon Capital of the World", Campbell River is located along the scenic Inside Passage on north central Vancouver Island. To the north is Robson Bight, the world's only Killer Whale sanctuary. Photo: Chris Cheadle

"Oh, I have slipped the surly bonds of earth
And danced the skies on laughter silvered wings;
Sunward I've climbed and joined the tumbling mirth
Of sun-split clouds - and done a hundred things
You have not dreamed of - wheeled and soared and swung
High in the sunlit silence. Hov'ring there,
I've chased the shouting wind along and flung
My eager craft through footless halls of air:
Up, up the long delirious, burning blue
I've topped the wind-swept heights with easy grace,
Where never lark, or even eagles, flew;
And, while with silent, lifting mind I've trod
The high untrespassed sanctity of space,
Put out my hand and touched the face of God."

John Gillespie Magee, Jr. 1941
*The 19 year-old, American born, RCAF Spitfire pilot whose sonnet, "In High Flight", was chosen as the official poem of the Royal Air Force and of the Royal Canadian Air Force. It was scribbled on the back of a letter written to his parents just days before he was killed in action on December 11th, 1941.*

*A nine-plane Diamond Formation of the famous 431 Air Demonstration Squadron, better known as the "Snowbirds", over the Comox Glacier on Vancouver Island.*

# Acknowledgments

## The Pilots

To all of you listed here, and to the few I have undoubtedly missed, many thanks for all those smooth flights, for making your flying machines do all the impossible things I asked of you, and for putting up with my interminable whining when the weather Gods turned my light off, Thank you one and all. Really!

| | |
|---|---|
| Jonathan Bouvier | Jason Mathieson |
| Wilf Bruce | Gary McClaskey |
| Marlene Cameron | Jody McRae |
| Saul Cartman | Dave Miller |
| Barry Cason | George Morrow |
| Shai Dubey | Henri Paris |
| Zoltan Duda | Tyler Pearson |
| Bob Elliot | Scott Pike |
| Trevor Erhardt | Eric Pootmans |
| Rastio Flogi | Ted Prinsen |
| Andre Fournier | Jaret Quiring |
| Mathieu Francoeur | Josh Robinson |
| Simon Garrett | Stu Somers |
| Gerry Gellner | Walt Somers |
| Steven Glasspool | Jonathan Steinfeld |
| David Guillemot | Bob Turner |
| Geordie Hachez | Phil Tweten |
| Dave Hopkins | Frank Valla |
| Chris Hrabb | Albert Vanderlay |
| Pamela Knight | Kevin Varey |
| Dan Knoop | Jim Vinacco |
| Richard Lafor | James Warankie |
| Fred Landry | Bob Willemsen |
| David Latour | Glen Young |
| Brian Legge | |

## The Photographers

A special thanks also to you who filled in the considerable gaps in my coverage. This is a far better book than it would have been without your wonderful images.

| | |
|---|---|
| Barrette & MacKay | Russ Heinl |
| Bela Baliko | Mia et Klaus |
| Mike Beedell | Jeanette Lightwood |
| Hans Blohm | Wayne Lynch |
| Chris Cheadle | |

## Your Turn

People lean towards the view that aerial photography is difficult, dangerous and best left to the professionals. Rubbish. If you take pictures on the ground and enjoy flying, why not take your camera for a photo flight?

My favourite photo platform is the reliable old Cessna 172. It has an overhead wing and is certified for flight with one door removed, although some pilots will not take the door off. If you encounter this problem, or feel uncomfortable flying with it off, the window will open up to the wing and provide almost the same freedom of view as having no door. The idea is to avoid shooting through window glass. The "172" is also very common in Canada. Most flying schools have one and will be happy to take you flying for a charter fee in the neighbourhood of $130.00 an hour. But you can cover a lot of ground in a typical photo flight of 30 to 40 minutes so it is not an overly expensive proposition.

## A Few Suggestions

By far the best lens is a zoom in the 35-70 range. Much wider and you will have a part of the wing, strut or wheel in the frame. Much longer and you will have sharpness problems. Use a 100 ASA film and a shutter speed of 1000th of a second or faster. Ask the pilot to fly at 1000 feet above the ground and have him slow down to around 70kts. when you are over your target. Things will go much smoother if you show him the area you are interested in on the map first. Ask for a headset so you can give him instructions to put you in the right piece of sky to get the shot you're after. Best bet is to fly a right hand orbit around your target so you will see it in a variety of different light – i.e. side, front and back lit. Avoid the temptation to brace yourself on the door edge. This will transmit the plane's vibration down your arm to the camera and give you sharpness problems. Also, try to keep the lens barrel inside the cabin as the slipstream will make it much more difficult to aim the camera and hold it steady. And keep an eye on the horizon to make sure it is level. Best time of day is early morning or late afternoon. Longer shadows are more interesting and will give your photos more "depth". If you are going up to shoot a particular building, make sure you go at a time of day when light hits the front facade. And, most important, if the door is off secure everything inside the aircraft and wrap your seatbelt buckle with duct tape. And that's the short course…

# Index